Praise for *Lessons from the Dying*

"Smith communicates such a deep trust in death that we, too,
as readers, start to regard death as a friend."
—*Inquiring Mind*

"Schooled in Buddhist meditation, Rodney brings clarity and a
straightforward approach to these 'lessons,' making them quite practical for the deepening of the mind as well as the broadening of the
heart. He offers to the dying first, and the rest of us by
association, an increase in loving presence."
—Stephen Levine, author of *Who Dies?*

"*Lessons from the Dying* is rooted in simple experience and keeps coming back persistently to the wisdom the dying have for us."
—*Tricycle: The Buddhist Review*

"A valuable collection of stories and meditations. These are not just
lessons from the dying; they are lessons for the living. A book that can
prepare us for our inevitable encounter with death."
—*East & West Series*

"Smith writes compellingly on the nature, value, and connection
between life and death. The dying have much to teach us about the
manner in which we could begin to live our lives anew. This book is an
eloquent, sensitive testimony by an individual who has deeply
considered this important, life-altering event."
—*The Beacon*

"Full of gems. One of the best books on death and dying
I have had the chance to read."
—*The Great Adventure*

"In this extraordinary volume, Rodney Smith opens our hearts, minds,
and souls to the great mystery we all must face."
—*Values & Visions*

LESSONS FROM THE DYING

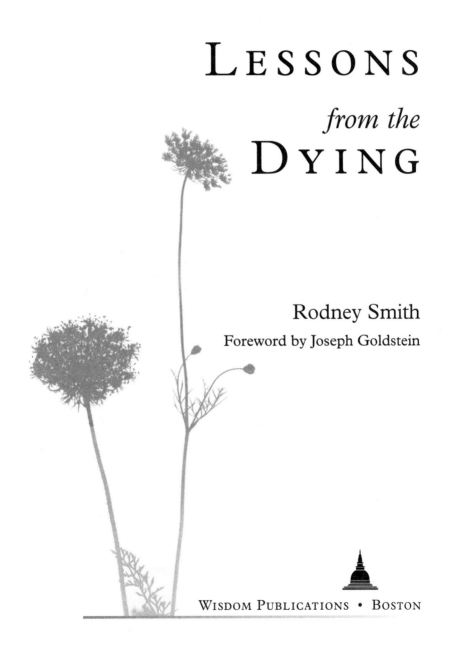

LESSONS
from the
DYING

Rodney Smith

Foreword by Joseph Goldstein

WISDOM PUBLICATIONS • BOSTON

Wisdom Publications
199 Elm Street
Somerville, MA 02144 USA
www.wisdompubs.org

Passage on p. 24 printed with the permission of Simon & Schuster from *Journey to Ixtlan* by Carlos Castaneda. Copyright © 1972 by Carlos Casteneda.
Epigraph on p. 7 from "Take a Giant Step" by Gerald Goffin and Carole King. © EMI Music Publishing. Sung by Taj Mahal on *The Best of Taj Mahal*. © 1981 CBS Inc.

Library of Congress Cataloging-in-Publication Data
Smith, Rodney (Teacher)
  Lessons from the dying / Rodney Smith ; foreword by Joseph Goldstein.—2 [edition].
    pages cm
  Includes bibliographical references.
  ISBN 1-61429-194-2 (pbk. : alk. paper)
  1. Death—Religious aspects. 2. Hospice care—Religious aspects. I. Title.
  BL504.S65 2015
  202'.3—dc23

                        2014016553

ISBN 9781614291947   ebook ISBN 9780861718917

19 18 17 16 15   5 4 3 2 1

Cover design by Phil Pascuzzo. Interior design by Gopa&Ted2, Inc.
Set in Plantin MT Pro 10.125/15.

Wisdom Publications' books are printed on acid-free paper and meet the guidelines for permanence and durability of the Production Guidelines for Book Longevity of the Council on Library Resources.

This book was produced with environmental mindfulness. We have elected to print this title on 30% PCW recycled paper. As a result, we have saved the following resources: 12 trees, 6 million BTUs of energy, 1,024 lbs. of greenhouse gases, 5,583 gallons of water, and 377 lbs. of solid waste. For more information, please visit our website, www.wisdompubs.org.

Printed in the United States of America.

Please visit www.fscus.org.

Rehearse death. To say this is to tell a person to rehearse his freedom. A person who has learned how to die has unlearned how to be a slave.

—SENECA, *Letters from a Stoic*

Contents

Foreword by Joseph Goldstein xiii

Acknowledgments xv

Introduction I
    My Journey   2
    About the Reflections and Exercises   4

1: Delighting in the Mystery 7
    The Intuitive Heart   II
    Appreciation and Joy   I3
    MYSTERY AND JOY   I6

2: Seeing Things as They Are I9
    Reflecting on Death   22
    OBSERVING RESISTANCE   29

3: Risking Our Lives 3I
    The Urgency to Change   33
    From Fear to Affection   37
    HABITS AND CHANGE   42

4: Acknowledging the Shadow 45
    Separating Life and Death   47
    The Meeting of Life and Death   50
    THE SHADOW   54

5: Being Human 57
    Dying as a Human Being   60
    Addressing Our Fears   63

Forgiveness 66
BEARING OUR HUMANITY 72

6: Learning from Every Experience 75
Using Life for Learning 77
The Known and the Unknown 82
Learning from Death 85
LEARNING FROM THE UNKNOWN 88

7: Listening from the Heart 91
Projections 93
Listening to the Dying 95
True and Useful 98
Intimacy 100
LISTENING AND SPEAKING 103

8: Searching for Meaning 107
Hope 110
The Relativity of Meaning 115
FINDING MEANING 121

9: Understanding Our Suffering 123
Understanding Suffering 126
In Conflict with Reality 130
BEFRIENDING PAIN 134

10: Opening Our Hearts 137
Finding Our Affection 139
The Caring Heart 142
Love and the Ego 147
LOVE, COMPASSION, AND INTIMACY 150

11: The Dying Mind 153
Denial 155
The Loss of Control 158
Losing Our Sense of Self 161

Trusting the Process   163
LETTING GO OF CONTROL   166

12: Understanding Grief   169
How We Grieve   171
Why We Grieve   174
Grief and Change   176
OPENING THE HEART TO GRIEF   178

13: The Ending of Time   181
Fractured Time   184
Integrating into Time Present   187
UNDERSTANDING YOUR RELATIONSHIP TO TIME   191

14: The Deathless   193
Living Our Death   195
From Death to the Deathless   197

Further Reading   203

About the Author   207

Foreword

IN *Lessons from the Dying*, Rodney Smith makes a meaningful offering to all of us interested in freedom. Drawing on an unusually rich array of experience, Rodney clearly elucidates the wisdom drawn from both his years as a Buddhist practitioner and monk and his long involvement in the hospice movement. Each of these deep wellsprings of his life enriches the other and finds expression in this helpful and inspiring book.

Lessons from the Dying could also be called "lessons for the living" because of the courageous honesty revealed in so many of the stories told here. These accounts reflect back to us our own attitudes toward death and love, and they prompt us to examine the way we are living our lives right now. In the busyness of our lives we rarely take the time to consider our mortality and the implications that it might have for the choices we make. Yet when we do cultivate this awareness it becomes a powerful force for wise discrimination.

Reflections on death are a transforming part of spiritual practice in many different traditions. These meditations remind us that life is transient and that, in the end, there is nothing we can hold on to, or truly call our own, except for the effects of our own actions. Our lives grow shorter, all accumulation ends in dispersion, all meetings in separation. Given these truths, at the time of death what would we most want to have accomplished in our lives? The time to ask this question is now, so that we can bring the wisdom of our values to bear on how we choose to live.

Rodney skillfully guides us through the subtleties and nuances of our own assumptions, hopes, and fears. He shows the possibility of living and dying with an open heart. *Lessons from the Dying* is a wise and gentle reminder of what faces us all, a reminder that death is the great mystery that illuminates life.

Joseph Goldstein

Acknowledgments

OCCASIONALLY PEOPLE APPEAR in our lives who lead us deeper into the mystery of life. Two such friends helped me open the door to death and dying. Once opened it has never closed. One was Marion Wilson, my first hospice director and a person who trusts totally in her heart and would never allow me to forget my own. The second was Paula Paust, my first director of social services. With Paula, it was like being on a journey with your best friend. We kept each other on our edge. We had countless discussions around all aspects of death and dying as we endlessly pursued the unknown.

My teachers of self-awareness are too many to list. To all I bow deeply with boundless gratitude. Special thanks to Joseph Goldstein, Sharon Salzberg, and Jack Kornfield who encouraged this work to completion.

A special thanks to Laura Croft and Tom Joyce who labored long and hard making important suggestions and editing this manuscript from beginning to end. Much gratitude to the following friends who helped throughout the project: Ellen McCown, Kody Janney, Eunice Nakao, and Roy Tribelhorn.

Introduction

Do you want to know what it is like to die?
Think of the thing you treasure the most and drop it!
That is death.

—J. KRISHNAMURTI

WHY WOULD WE WANT to approach the subject of death? Why not leave it alone until we are forced by circumstances to face it? When Sir Edmund Hillary, the first person to climb Mount Everest, was questioned by a reporter who wanted to understand what had motivated him to climb the peak, Hillary is said to have replied, "Because it is there." So too is our death. It is there ... and it will not go away. When we avoid the subject it works its terror below our awareness until we consciously begin our ascent. As we climb we begin to see life from a different perspective, and we eventually open to a full view of freedom.

Books on every facet of death and dying have been written, from near-death experiences to navigational guides through the after-death portal. Universities now routinely offer courses of intensive study on death and dying. We have become more comfortable with the death-related titles in bookstores, more at ease with the obituary column in the newspaper, and are at last beginning to include the subject as a topic for serious conversation.

Nevertheless, the overall impact of this death-related activity has been minor. One reason is because study does not necessarily translate into personal change. Writing books and offering university courses can be the first indication that a subject is receiving the attention it deserves, but death requires much more from us than academic learning. When we read about death it remains distant, something that happens to other people. Our lives seem more secure than the lives of the dying on the pages of a book. We cannot play with death as an intellectual curiosity and expect it to reveal its secrets.

We find ourselves both approaching and avoiding the subject. We want to move closer to the topic as long as we can apply Woody Allen's rule, "I don't mind dying. I just don't want to be around when it happens." A wide gap lies between recognizing the subject and letting it into our hearts. If we are to be altered by death, we must give it our full attention. This means reflecting on it and learning its lessons. When we allow ourselves to learn from death, the psychic distance between those who are dying and those who are healthy narrows. We see that health is simply a phase of the life cycle that will inevitably be followed by the final phase, physical death.

MY JOURNEY

My own odyssey with death began as a Buddhist monk in the forests of Thailand. After living apart from others for a number of years, first in a lay monastery in the West and later in the Thai forest monastery, my meditation practice started to feel a little dry. The dryness seemed to be coming from a part of me that was not being nourished by my solitary monk's life. I did not completely understand why my heart was backing away from this isolation. Living alone had allowed me an intimate understanding of who I was, as well as of the nature of life itself. Now something was pulling me away from this reclusiveness in an unknown direction.

Around this same time I read Stephen Levine's book *Who Dies?* The book clarified the dependence between conscious living and conscious dying. My heart connected immediately with the possibilities of working with the dying as a continuation of my spiritual work. Here was a solution to the dryness of my heart; here was a way to work with people that was as intense and focused as the years of formal meditation.

I disrobed as a monk in 1983, returned to the United States, and began my career as a full-time hospice worker. I have had many different positions in hospice work including social worker, bereavement coordinator, volunteer trainer, director of social services, clinical director, and executive director. Each position has given me a distinct perspective on the dying process. Learning has come not only from the patients and families but also from the hospice staff, whose caring and compassionate hearts have set a standard for the health care field. All of us who work with the dying are like little children who have gathered together for solace as we attempt to decipher the code of life.

Death has been an extraordinary teacher. Now after years of hospice work I am still as mystified about death as I was many years ago in the forest. The subject eludes closure and resolution. I have become familiar with how people die, and I am enriched by the lessons the dying have imparted, but what death is remains a mystery. My training will never be completed.

Investigating death has unveiled revelation after revelation. It has led me into the dark corners of my shadow, where I lost sight of my wholeness. It has allowed life to open into a profound sense of joy and appreciation. I do not know whether I will ever be completely comfortable with my own dying, but I do know that I am less afraid to be who I am. I attribute this to attuning myself to the lessons of the dying. Understanding these lessons has become a private and personal pilgrimage into the holiness of life.

Although the pages of this book are filled with hospice stories, the stories are about you and me, for every one of us is a hospice patient. The stories evoke our own patterns, fears, and wisdom. If we substitute ourselves for the patients, we begin to understand experientially the way we limit ourselves, the way we hold ourselves back, the way we rest in safety at the expense of a greater freedom available to us all. We do not have to wait to become ill for the message of the dying to reflect our vulnerability. Our fears echo throughout the entire corridor of our lives from birth to death.

Joseph Campbell said that the real search is not for the meaning of life but for the experience of being alive. Ironically, the lessons of the dying point to this end. Many of the terminally ill become acutely alive during their dying. They realize that time is sacred and that they can no longer postpone their living. They wake up to the variety and expressions of life that they had taken for granted.

Physical death is a metaphor for the death of all experience. It encompasses the ending not only of the body but of all life experience. Small deaths occur to us throughout the day. Each time our expectations are not realized, we die to our ideals. Every time we attempt to freeze a moment in time we are faced with the limits of our control and the death of our influence. Whenever we hold on to any aspect of life and it evolves into something else, we are left with our despair. Since many of our psychological difficulties come from how we handle transitions, death provides understanding into how and why we suffer. A deep and penetrating awareness of death gives direct insight into most of our problems. To investigate death, then, is to comprehend our confusion and ignorance of life.

Actual patients who have confronted their death, and whose dying experiences I relate here, are the heroes in my life and in my book. But although their tales may entice and fascinate, we may also find ourselves psychologically distant. Then we know we have pulled back from the subject and allowed ourselves to read it as if it were happening only to them, not to us. This is a "happening to me" book. The reflections and exercises at the end of each chapter are intended to bring the points of each section home. They are experiential exercises that give the insights realistic impact.

Death is here. It is a frontier that few of us willfully cross. This book offers us an opportunity to engage—and perhaps struggle—with a subject that has lain dormant far too long. Its focus is to provide a unique intimacy with the lessons surrounding death. We are all going to die. What do we have to lose by addressing the subject now? Perhaps a new life is waiting for those courageous enough to open to its teachings.

ABOUT THE REFLECTIONS AND EXERCISES

If your life has not been touched by death or dying, it can be very difficult to understand the lessons that death teaches. The following chapters are meant to bring you to that understanding. The stories in them will allow you to glimpse how others have feared, coped with, and even welcomed death. But to integrate the experiences of the dying with your own requires more than merely reading this book. It requires that you go through similar experiences as well.

Each chapter discusses one of the many lessons that the dying communicate. At the end of each discussion, a set of reflections and exercises aims to transform the key ideas into insight and understanding. It is insight that will change your actions and be of benefit to your life. Reading a chapter without putting it into practice may open you to the topic of death, but it will not effect long-term change. Reading allows you to mull over the words and entertain new ideas; practicing these ideas changes the way you perceive the world and opens you beyond your fears.

It is not easy to practice and reflect upon these themes. Be gentle with yourself as you approach each exercise. Be aware of the power of working with death. If you find yourself in a weakened mental or physical state, it is probably better to pull back from these exercises and reengage when you feel empowered to do so. Let your heart be your guide. It is not a question of waiting until the exercises become easy in order to involve yourself with them. They will never be easy or pleasant as long as there is resistance. The unpleasantness is an indication of your need to practice.

If you have a tendency to feel unworthy about yourself, these exercises may reinforce that pattern. It is important to use them wisely. If, for example, in a particular exercise you are reflecting on a personal attribute such as fear and how it controls your life, you could become very judgmental of all the ways you are afraid. This attitude only reinforces your self-criticism. Try approaching self-knowledge through kindness toward yourself. Kindness allows whatever you are observing to be seen without relating it back to your old conditioning. With practice, kindness can become the foundation for all self-observations.

If you become frustrated and annoyed, stop the exercise. Instead of reflecting on yourself apply the exercise to other people. If you observe them, you will find that many people share your patterns of aversions and avoidances. Then return to self-observation and reconnect with the exercise, allowing your heart to remain open to everyone's suffering. This will allow you to have a little more space around this habit pattern and not take it so personally. It will also give you more resolve to understand it, for you will see how your understanding opens your heart to a compassionate response and directly influences the shared pain we all have around death and dying.

The easiest way to work with these reflections and exercises is to give yourself a designated period of time each day. Sit comfortably and read each reflection (printed in italics) slowly until one resonates with you. Then work with the accompanying exercise. Spend some time alone working with the words. If you are confused about what the exercise is asking, search back through that chapter for guidance and clarity. If it still does not make sense, skip it and go to the next. Once you have understood the purpose of the exercise, you can carry it throughout the day, allowing it to integrate into your perceptions.

Each chapter can stand alone or be read in sequence. You can never really finish working with the exercises. Each time you return to them, you move more deeply into the experience. It is a never-ending adventure into the truth of who you are and your relationship with life and death.

1 | Delighting in the Mystery

*Do you remember as a child when you woke up
and morning smiled? It's time, it's time, it's time
we felt like that again.*
—TAJ MAHAL

FOR THOSE WHO ARE WILLING to learn, the dying offer
powerful lessons on how to live with vitality and passion. Most of us do
not give death the attention it deserves, and the lessons go unheeded.
Every contact with death has the potential to deepen our understanding
of life regardless of whether there is a peaceful resolution or an intense
and dramatic struggle.

As a hospice worker and student of the dying, I have been given
glimpses of the insights people gain as they face the loss of all they have
ever known. Fundamental to all these interactions has been a profound
confrontation with the mystery of life and death. This mystery is inherent in being alive. Each of us knew it once, but somehow it became lost
as we pursued other interests.

Most of us remember the excitement of childhood. We would wake
up with our heads swirling in a magical world rich with possibilities.
Each rock in a stream, each cloud in the sky, held a secret or a surprise.
The world was a stage for our learning and growth. We hungered for the
answers and used all expressions of life as our teachers.

As we grew, the potential of the world narrowed under the influence
of more formal lessons. Our minds were directed toward a logical and
scientific view. Everything happened from reasonable causes and predictable effects. There was no place left for the inexplicable. We were told
that with enough study the universe could be thoroughly understood.
One of the implicit directives of our early education was for everyone to
see things from the same perspective. This helped to establish common

group values and norms, but it robbed us of the capacity to see life from any other perspective than how we were taught—and that eliminated much of the mystery.

I grew up playing with a friend in an imaginative world of thieves and white knights. Hour after hour we created scenes of destruction only to be saved in the nick of time by one brave warrior or another. One day my friend refused to play. The game could not be played alone, so I coaxed and pleaded with him to continue, but he was steadfast. I remember asking my friend why he suddenly decided to stop playing what had always been such imaginative fun for both of us. His answer has stayed with me to this day. He said he had mentioned the game to his father and had been told to stop all of that foolishness and grow up. We never played the game again, and I remember grieving deeply the loss of that world.

Is it possible to reawaken to the mystery of the world? This mystery does not lie in the hidden recesses of our imagination or in long-lost childhood games. It lies immediately before us. The mystery has never left the world; we have left it. We have done so by accepting the conventional ways we've been taught to think and experience. Sometimes people who are dying allow the mystery to return. They reacquire the innocent eyes of youth, and the mystery unfolds before them.

One hospice patient spoke about her view of the world as she was dying: "I wake up after a night sleep and check myself to see if I am still alive. Yes, today I can still hear and see. I can't take anything for granted anymore. But when I look around the room at things that I have lived with my whole life, everything looks a little different. Objects have taken on a shine and a newness as if I had never seen them before. Everything is both familiar and unfamiliar at the same time."

When we examine something as familiar as a leaf and study it closely, we find that we actually understand very little about it. We may know what tree it fell from, its form, shape, and color, but nothing about what it is. A botanist or a physicist could tell us a great deal about the details of a leaf but very little about its essence. Despite much scientific research and exploration, no one knows what a single thing is.

Just because we can give an object a name does not mean that we understand it; its essence will always escape attempts to define it. If we do not get lost in the name and description, however, everything—from the smallest leaf to the remotest star—opens up into a question.

Consider the question of what it means to be a human being. Birth and death are the boundaries of our known existence and embody the enigma of life. We attempt to understand who we are by investigating where we came from and where we are going. This is one of the reasons that death holds such a fascination for us. By approaching it we hope to gain insight into our real nature, but that nature is as unfathomable as death itself. We must attempt to understand death even in the face of its incomprehensibility. Even though our minds are comfortable only in the security of the known, the creative and intuitive side of us thrives when we encounter the mysterious. So the mind works to make death understandable even as our hearts delight with the impossibility of the task.

Meeting the mysterious can shatter our usual perspective on life. One of our hospice nurses tells the story of a patient named Jim who was very close to the end of his life. Unknown to Jim, his brother died suddenly in a car accident. In a room far away from the patient, the hospice nurse and the family discussed whether Jim should be told about his brother's death. Together they decided that it was probably better not to disturb him with this news given the fact that he was very close to death. The family felt the news would cause him unnecessary stress at a time when he needed his mind to be as clear as possible. The family and the nurse then entered the room where Jim was coming out of a coma. As they entered, Jim rose up on his elbows and asked why no one had told him that his brother had died. The family, astonished, asked him how he knew. He said he had been speaking with his brother in the tunnel. Jim then laid back and died.

Our hearts love stories such as these because some fundamental part of ourselves is confirmed. If we have a very strong intellect or a firm need for security, however, such stories may provoke cynicism. Then the mind overrules the heart's need to dwell in wonder, and we find ourselves overreacting and becoming defensive whenever we attempt to resolve conflicting parts within ourselves. The mind believes only what it sees as logical and interprets death as simply the ending of the mind-body process. Separated from the heart, the mind becomes spiritually dry, unable to find wonder in what the intellect cannot explain.

My father was a scientist and religious skeptic for most of his life. He would counter Christian miracle stories with scientific explanations or dismiss them as exaggerations. About ten years before his own death, his wife of thirty years died suddenly and unexpectedly. He was deeply torn with grief. Years later he confided in me that something miraculous had happened to him right after my mother died. He said she had come to him, touched him on the arm, and whispered in his ear that she was very sorry to have left him but that he would make it through this grief and eventually heal. He said he did not know how to explain it, but it had happened, and he knew from that day forth that there was something else to life and death that science could not explain.

My mother's visit called into question my father's rational world. What was surprising to those of us who knew my father's scientific focus was the degree of certainty with which he accepted this event, whose meaning was experiential, not anecdotal. Through this experience his conviction in the mysterious became unshakable. This event took him beyond theory, beyond his mind, and touched his heart. His heart told him that he had been mistaken in the past. Life contained more than he ever imagined.

Perhaps experiencing mystery directly is necessary to shake our perspective on reality. Many times while working with the dying I have been thrown into a different view of reality. I have looked into their eyes and watched as they communicated with things unseen and reached out to touch something invisible, while their lips moved in silent speech. During those moments I knew there was much more to reality than our limited senses could perceive.

A medical director at a hospice where I worked was tending to a dying patient in the patient's home. The patient, who was sitting on a couch and speaking coherently, suddenly fell silent. The doctor looked at the patient and peered deeply into his eyes. The patient died that very moment and through his gaze pulled the doctor with him to the edge of death. When the doctor retold the story to the rest of us at our hospice team meeting, he said, "His stare took me to the edge of my own life. His gaze was without end. There was nobody there, just infinite space."

The dying may allow us to understand ourselves more clearly, but we do not need to be dependent on a particular event in life to communicate this mystery. In fact, we are in immediate contact with it at all times. Everyone can touch and experience it firsthand in this very moment. The breeze on our cheeks, the smell of a flower, a tree swaying in the wind, all are miracle stories. If we could assume the lost innocence of our youth these miraculous events would be obvious to us all.

We can look at miracle stories as an extension of this view of innocence. One interpretation of Christ's miracles is that they call us to look beyond what we know. Maybe Christ was demonstrating through miracles what was always before his eyes. He might have been saying that everything is continuously a miracle, that we all have the potential to change the ordinary into the extraordinary, and that the Kingdom of God is at hand in our everyday world. Each and every object is then a gateway to the miraculous.

THE INTUITIVE HEART

Being present at a birth or death frequently leaves us with a sense of wonder and awe. Where does life come from? At death, where does it go? Standing by the bed of someone who is dying or giving birth, we can feel like little children in a world of unlimited possibilities. Our minds are watching and listening intently; we are focused and attentive, not thinking in a preset way. We are uncluttered with definitions or agendas. Our hearts are wide open, and our minds are not cluttered with thought. This is the realm of the intuitive heart.

I was the social worker for Jane, a hospice patient who was living with her daughter, Susan. On one of my visits, I was speaking with Susan when I looked over her shoulder and saw her mother in bed. As I was watching Jane, something alerted me to the fact that she was beginning to actively die. I was about to say this to the daughter when the phone rang, and Susan left the room to answer it. I got up and moved closer to the dying patient. Seeing that my suspicions were correct, I started to turn and alert the daughter who was still on the phone. Something stopped me, and I thought, "No, this woman needs to die without her daughter being present." Jane died, and Susan finished her conversation and walked back to where I was standing. When I told her that her mother had just died, Susan blurted out, "Thank God I wasn't in the room to see that! I could not have stood it, and my mother would not have wanted me there!"

When we act from intuition we have become part of the mystery. We frequently cannot say why we acted in a particular way. We just did it because it was appropriate given the clarity with which we were seeing the situation in front of us, in all of its parts, as a singular experience. The intuitive response acknowledges the wholeness of our perception. Our comprehension is as spacious as the entire environment. When all the pieces are seen with clarity, our heart moves us in an appropriate way.

Acting on the intuitive impulses of the heart can be confusing. It takes practice to recognize the difference between our heart speaking and our mind telling us it is our heart speaking. For example, many times as a hospice social worker I would be passing a home of one of my patients when I would suddenly have an impulse to stop and visit that patient rather than continuing on to my destination. Usually I would dismiss this urge as a distraction and convince myself it was just a random thought. On returning to the hospice I would occasionally discover the patient had died around the time this thought had occurred to me. On one occasion I remember returning to hear the family had been in trouble and had attempted to contact me at exactly this same time.

After a few of these situations, I decided I would stop whenever the impulse occurred. I started to look for that intuitive feeling and probably subconsciously created the thought. But after I had made the decision to stop, I usually found that there was nothing going on with the patient or the family. It seemed that when I tried to force or control the intuition, it vanished. Intuition, I discovered, was a part of the mystery of being and was better left alone.

A close friend and fellow hospice worker was excellent in predicting exactly when a patient was going to die. She always seemed to know the day and usually the hour when death would occur. I was intrigued with her accuracy and asked her to closely observe the signs she was seeing in the patient that led to these predictions. She did this for a while and soon became frustrated. She said when she tried to figure out what was occurring she would lose the intuition that allowed her to know when death was approaching. Her attempt to decipher her intuition was obscuring the premonition itself. Her accuracy fell dramatically and continued to fall the more she tried to regain her skill.

Clearly there is a way of knowing that is not based on discursive reasoning, but when we attempt to discover or find its source, the mystery recedes or vanishes. Mystery cannot be found within the range of what we know or what we think. We contact it through our hearts, not through our minds. This can be unsettling because our hearts offer us no explanation. The heart does not base itself in the security of our words. If we reach to grasp the heart, we find only space; if we seek to locate it, we find it everywhere and nowhere.

APPRECIATION AND JOY

A forty-seven-year-old hospice patient looked out of her window at the ocean, glistening in the morning sun. After quietly observing the view for a long time, she finally said, "Having grown up in this house, I have seen the sun shine on the water many times, but I have never appreciated it as I do now. Seeing it like this brings me a great deal of joy."

At one time or another we have all been too busy to notice the beauty before our eyes. We find ourselves moving too quickly through an event, not really seeing it at all, rushing on toward the next thing we have to do. We usually look through the present toward an idea about where we are going. This leaves us feeling unsettled in this moment as we reach to grasp the next. But when we are dying, we may find it difficult to ignore the immediate beauty of the now. We appreciate life because we have precious little time left to live and nowhere else we have to go.

Joy is the companion of the mysterious. It is undefined, wide open, and unbound to time and space. When we realize our time is limited, we consciously choose to stop and look around. We take the time to locate ourselves, and our hearts respond with spontaneous appreciation and joy. In the simple act of slowing down and being aware, we allow life to interact with our senses. With affectionate appreciation we unite with the wonder that has always been right before our eyes.

If we were fully aware that our breaths are numbered, how would we relate to the breath that we are taking right now? We would not take it for granted because we could not be sure that there would be another. Breathing would become a precious link to our life. The fact is our breaths are limited, regardless of our health, and through realizing this we have the opportunity to take more joy in how we spend them. Suppose we were born crippled and could suddenly walk. After all the years in a wheelchair, the smallest movement of our legs would certainly give us unfathomable joy. Can we experience that same joy now, when we are healthy and jogging with our breath fluid and effortless?

The simple movement of the body, the sound of a bird, the warmth of the sun—these are but a few of the many occasions we all have to come face to face with wonder in a deep and joyful way. If our senses are alive and awake, the world leaves an indelible mark in each moment. Nothing is passed over as irrelevant. Everything becomes appreciated for its own sake.

Too many of us for too long have appreciated the world from the pleasure that objects give us, not from the inherent beauty contained in the moment. We value objects that have helped us in the past or promise to do so in the future. But real appreciation rests within the moment itself, just for being how it is. When we focus on how useful something is, we miss its immediate radiance. Its shine is deflected into an imaginary time when we can use the object in a meaningful way.

When we realize that because we are dying, we do not have the luxury to extend ourselves beyond this moment, the mystery makes itself known, and our hearts become open and sensitive. Every experience affects us. We feel the richness of life—always incomprehensible, interesting, and unknowable. Since who we are is part of life, this wonder is inherently within us; it is waiting only for our acknowledgment. There is no need to cultivate it.

This wonder is not something to fear; it is a call to play and to express ourselves through unmistakable joy. It is the play of forming angels in the snow. We are grounded and in touch with our minds and bodies, but we are connected with the mystery beyond and through all forms. All things are what they are but also much more. The opportunities that life offers are not limited to our knowledge but hold unlimited possibilities. Our creativity and intuition access the endless magic. Everything affects our heart with the intimacy of a new love. It feels as if we are returning home.

Mystery and Joy

Before proceeding, you may wish to reread "About the Reflections and Exercises" in the introduction. This part of the chapter bridges the intellectual understanding that comes from reading and the transformation that occurs when you make the words your own. It is an integral part of this book.

* * *

Reflect on what you actually know about the world around you. You know its name, color, shape, utility, and history. But what about its essence? Science subdivides the world into smaller and smaller components, giving names and descriptions to each. But it never explains what a single thing actually is. Science may satisfy your mind's need to identify and locate the world, but what about your heart's yearning to rejoin the mystery? Are these two in conflict?

Study any object—a stone, a flower, a cup, your hand—allow the knowledge you have of it to surface but not define it. Look at it with a childlike mind as if you were viewing it for the first time. What do you see that is new? Do your new discoveries influence how you see the object? Can you continue to view the object without allowing it to be contaminated by this new information?

Reflect on how much creativity and spontaneity exist in your life. You can see mystery and wonder only when you are not acting from your old conditioned patterns. How bound are you to the views you hold? Can you sense the limitations of seeing things from an established perspective? Do your views interfere with being spontaneous?

Engage in a creative activity, such as painting, writing, cooking, or gardening. Watch yourself and try to notice when you are most creative and spontaneous. Then try to intentionally be creative and see what happens. What is necessary for creativity to arise?

Reflect on how much play, joy, and appreciation you have. Is life so focused on daily tasks that you can no longer enjoy the touch of a breeze on your cheek or the song of a bird? How does the "doing mind" keep you from experiencing life in a fuller way?

Sit for ten minutes each day and simply listen to the sounds of nature. Turn off your radio or TV and try to reserve some alone time. Remove all means of distraction. Without trying to identify the sounds or judge them in any way, listen to them as they arise from and fall back into silence. Feel the expression of joy and affection in your heart as you connect with the natural world. What is the relationship of that joy with the mystery of life?

2 | Seeing Things as They Are

*Life is so fragile, no more than a bubble blown to and fro
by the wind. How astonishing to think that after an
out-breath there will be an in-breath, or that we will
awaken after a night's sleep.*

—NAGARJUNA

MYSTERY MAKES ITSELF KNOWN when we begin to include death in our lives. It is as if a veil were lifted, allowing us to see clearly. Death is the way it has always been; we have just refused to acknowledge it. When we are able to see things as they are, we begin to tap our intuitive sense of the mysterious, and joy and appreciation grow. This process builds upon itself as we discover all the ways we hide from life.

As we have seen, the death experiences of others can teach us a great deal about how to live. By contemplating our own death we can learn even more. Imagine for a moment that it is time for you to die. Bring your awareness to this moment to see what your death can teach you about how to live. Will your hardened character patterns allow a peaceful or a difficult death? You can construct your own scene or use the following scenario.

It is the end of my life. I know I am dying. My relatives have gathered, and I appreciate the warmth and love that is being shown. I can tangibly feel the caring. My breath is erratic and labored. Everyone is talking about me, but not to me, as if I could no longer hear. Although I am unable to respond, my attention and focus are immediate. They say I am in a coma, but I know what is happening around me even though I cannot open my eyes. In this moment the purpose of life is so obvious. All of my possessions, status, and money are not helping me in this transition. My ambition and selfishness have offered me nothing that helps me to meet this moment with openness and understanding. How could I have been so blind not to have seen the limits of my lifestyle? The way to live has always been right before my eyes.

We all know intellectually that we are going to die. We usually see the event as something remote, occurring in a timely sequence after our body is old and depleted. Most of us see little value in studying the subject firsthand. "What is there to gain by such morbid reflections?" we may ask. "There is too much life to live! My death will occur in its own time anyway. I will give it my attention when I am forced to. Until then I'd rather dismiss it."

We labor under the delusion that life can be better served by removing death from view. Reflecting on death depresses us. We consider the pain of birth an occasion for celebration, but the suffering around death has little redeeming value. Grief is best left to the privacy of our homes. We encourage the bereaved to get on with their lives as soon as possible because we feel uneasy or awkward in the face of loss. We do not know what to say or how to comfort.

By reflecting on our personal history many of us will understand the immediacy of death. Most of us have come close to dying in one incident or another in our past. The car that almost hit us, the near drowning accident, the fall from the ladder, or the neighborhood robbery hold clues to the fragility of life. The Buddhist scriptures say, "Just as an arrow skillfully shot by an archer quickly reaches its target, so do our human lives." Life is a one-way road that moves with certainty toward its conclusion.

The idea that we or someone close to us may die usually causes a great deal of discomfort. The root of this disturbance is avoiding or rejecting the entire cycle of life. Many of us would prefer that life did not contain tragedy, discomfort, suffering, despondency, or death. We often conceive these as setbacks or deviations from what life is really about, which is happiness, health, and doing what we enjoy.

We feel that the world would be much improved if everything would go according to our moral views. Big fish should not eat small fish, and a kind heart should not have to suffer like the criminal. An honorable world would have the lives of the unjust ending sooner than the righteous, and children never dying before their parents.

But this is not the way things are. From a moral perspective death makes no sense at all. It does not build upon our accomplishments nor does it give credit for good intentions. Death throws into question the logic of our God. It has no morality and ignores our self-righteousness. It does not respond to our ideas of fairness. Death shatters our righteous ideas about fairness because it operates outside of that law. Death takes us all regardless of our past actions and reminds us constantly that we never have the upper hand. Its presence suggests that everything is fundamentally out of control.

The problem may not be with death but with our ideas about life. Sherlock Holmes use to say that if a clue did not fit the theory, throw away the theory, not the fact. But most of us do the opposite, we make every attempt to discard the fact of our death and make life meaningful on our own terms. We perpetuate the struggle with the facts of life because to acquiesce leaves us with little hope and no meaning. When we include death our world seems without purpose or direction. Most religions exist to create meaning out of the senselessness of death.

Our discomfort with death is one obvious indication that we are living at the expense of what is true. Death is a call to integrate the polar opposites: life and death, gain and loss, happiness and unhappiness, fame and disrepute, and pleasure and pain. When we seek one and avoid the other, we become a prisoner to both. Pleasure and pain are inescapable components of the whole of life. Pain causes us to suffer only when we struggle to maintain its opposite.

This problem arises in many situations throughout the day. For example, we have planned a picnic for Saturday. We wake up on Saturday morning to discover it is raining. We are very disappointed that the picnic must be canceled. Our desire for the situation to be different leads to our mental unrest. The longer we maintain the desire, the more we struggle. It is raining; that is the fact. We simply refuse to live according to that truth. We attempt to cover the facts of our life with our own projected memories. We create the polar opposite not from reality but from our imagination.

When I was a graduate student in social work my housemate was in her final phase of a terminal illness. I could feel how she wanted me to be available to her. She wanted someone to understand her pain. I had a very difficult time acknowledging her condition. All I wanted was to leave the house, and I would spend as much time away as possible. There I was, going to class learning how to be an empathetic listener while doing everything I could to escape the person who most needed someone to understand her! I could not face her because I wanted my life to be free of any reminder of death. I was running not only from her but from reality.

Death is the way things are. We can struggle with it, ignore it, repress it, try to ward it off with prayer; but there is nothing that will keep it from occurring. When we have used all means possible to keep death at bay and it still arrives on our threshold, then the only thing we can do is befriend it. We do it as the last alternative after we have tired from our futile avoidance. We do it because sooner or later reality comes crashing through our imagination.

Somewhere along the line it must dawn on us that to live in peace and contentment requires a radically different approach. Life must be lived according to its provisions, exactly how it is. In doing so there is the potential to harmonize with it rather than wage this senseless struggle. When we open to the truth the battle is over; but this does not mean we fall into despair. Most people discover that this "surrender" brings a renewed appetite for life and a growing serenity and open-hearted response to all experiences.

REFLECTING ON DEATH

There is a Buddhist story about a young woman whose child dies suddenly. She is so grieved she refuses to believe that her child is dead, and she travels to many of the well-known physicians of the time asking them to heal her son. The doctors keep telling her that her son has died, but she refuses to believe them. Finally out of frustration one doctor sends her to the Buddha. The Buddha tells the woman he will heal her dead son on one condition. She must go to the village and bring back a mustard seed from a family who has never been touched by death. People in India during that time lived in extended families. All the people who answered her request told her they had experienced many deaths over the years. In this way the woman realized that everyone must die and allowed her child to be buried.

Unlike this young woman most of us do not have such an intense denial of death. We know we are going to die. We just do not believe it will happen anytime soon. We stretch our tomorrows into an endless future. It is the immediacy of death, not death itself, that many of us fervently deny. Even the elderly who are terminally ill sometimes rage at the timing. I have worked with many eighty- and ninety-year-old terminally ill patients who felt it was unfair and untimely that they were having to die. It is difficult for most of us at any age to picture a world continuing without "me."

In a recent documentary on the January 17, 1995, earthquake in Kobe, Japan, one survivor recalled her own story: "I was in bed. It was about 5:45 A.M. Suddenly everything started shaking. The earth turned to liquid. Glass shattered all around my bed. I tried to stand up but realized the ceiling was on my head. My house had collapsed around me and buried me under the roof and walls. I remember yelling and yelling, but no one came. Then everything went dark. The next thing that I remember was a doctor standing over me. I was covered in blood." Over five thousand people died that day. It was a day just like today.

When I was a monk in Thailand I would occasionally go to the local hospital and view autopsies. I would go there to balance my understanding of the body as being both beautiful and unpleasant and to impassion a sense of urgency toward seeing things as they are. Because I had been meditating for a number of years, my mind was relatively quiet. Frequently when I was viewing these cadavers, many of whom had been dead for only a few hours, I could feel the deceased's consciousness hovering close by. It was as if the consciousness were confused about whether it was still alive. There had been little or no preparation for the death. Suddenly the consciousness had been severed from the body without explanation. Without anticipation a person's life had suddenly come to an end.

It is important to face the fact that life can end at any time. The realization that death is imminent empowers us to use our remaining time well. It takes away our excuses and forces us to take responsibility. We do what is appropriate because we cannot delay. Such contemplation allows our activities to be infused with personal integrity.

The Yaqui sorcerer Don Juan says to Carlos Castaneda in *Journey to Ixtlan*: "We don't have time, my friend, that is the misfortune of human beings. Focus your attention on the link between you and your death without remorse or sadness or worrying. Focus your attention on the fact that you don't have time and let your acts flow accordingly. Let each of your acts be your last battle on earth. Only under those conditions will your acts have their rightful power. Otherwise they will be, for as long as you live, the acts of a timid man." Carlos asks if it is so terrible to be a timid person, and Don Juan responds, "No. It isn't if you are going to be immortal, but if you are going to die there is no time for timidity, simply because timidity makes you cling to something that exists only in your thoughts. It soothes you while everything is at a lull, but then the awesome, mysterious world will open its mouth for you, as it will open for every one of us, and you will realize your sure ways were not sure at all."

Sometimes the event that triggers a serious reflection of our own ending is the dying of a close relative or friend. We can no longer deny death's presence by skipping over the obituary column or changing the subject when death arises in conversation. Though the pain in our heart is intense, our involvement with the family counters our need to escape. We care how the dying person is doing, how the spouse is adjusting to the illness, and whether the family will do well after the death. We see the dying person and compare her position with our own. "It could have been me. I am close to that age. She was in such good health, and now suddenly she is dying."

And then all too often sleep once again covers our eyes, and we slumber in a world that lives forever. Our fear of death fogs our view of life as it is. If we reflect upon it at all, we attempt to keep the issue "out there," happening to someone else. Because we try to hide from the impact of our death, we are often left with a free-floating anxiety. Contact with a dying friend can shake the psyche, but instead of using that experience to open to the paradoxes of life we frequently recoil in fear. A brush with death can make us more protective and insecure with our own family, or it can leave us with a pervasive sense of self-concern. We find that we are overly anxious when our son or daughter is late returning home, or we become overly focused on our own aging.

Even hospice staff who work daily with the terminally ill have difficulty carrying the impact of that work into the rest of their lives. It is easier to allow the dying person into our hearts than the dying process. The hospice worker sometimes develops a mechanical routine that allows her to be effective on her job but detached and untouched by the fact of dying. It is hard to stay awake to death. We are not used to including it in our thoughts. One hospice worker summed it up: "I have to wake up to my death every day to be effective in this job."

It is difficult for a physically healthy person to get very close to death. Beyond a certain point we cannot know what it is like to die. The truth of the process will remain essentially unknown until we are involved with it directly. Reading about death or attending to a dying patient can allow us to feel secure in the knowledge of how someone dies, and empathetically we can approach the patient's inner struggle; but what it is really like to lose everything in the world cannot be understood until it occurs.

However, the fact that we cannot know what death is until it occurs should not keep us from continually exploring it. One of the values of reflecting on death is that it allows us to work with the edge of our fears. It keeps us moving along with life so that we do not get stuck.

No matter how knowledgeable we feel about death, there is always more to learn. We think we have journeyed as far as the subject can take us, and then suddenly through tragedy or illness we discover we have been held in check by our fear. We begin to understand that death will never let us rest; there is always more to learn.

An experienced hospice nurse developed a lump in her breast and went to the doctor for an evaluation. She later said that the time between the examination and being told that the lump was benign showed her how far she actually lived from the experience of a hospice patient. She said her fear was overwhelming. She had renewed appreciation for what her patients go through every day. She had worked hard over the years to open to the dying process, but her fear revealed that she remained an outsider. She said she had seen hundreds of patients die and had always assumed she understood what the patient and family went through. This false understanding had given her a certain security. Her previous assumptions were really an expression of her need to make dying safe. Her work with the dying had been shaped by her fear of the very process she was attempting to understand. Death, she concluded, would never allow her the luxury of resting on what she already knew.

Many of us have an abiding interest in death and dying even as we actively try to exclude it from our world view. The many books that have been written regarding life after clinical death have stirred our interest in the possibilities of what that moment may offer. We look to such books and to our religious teachings for safety and structure in that fearful, unknowable moment.

We close down around all living experiences when we are afraid of dying. We protect ourselves from the entire expanse and mystery of life by shaving off the parts we do not like. We imagine we can have life on our own terms: the good without the bad, pleasure free of pain, happiness unaccompanied by sorrow, and life free of imminent death. But one defines the other and is inseparable from it. Immediate and momentary life requires the inclusion of a sudden impending death. Only by accessing the mystery of both worlds do we become complete.

Occasionally the pain of dying or the grief from losing loved ones leaves us traumatized. We feel so frightened from the experience that we back away from our emotions and stay frozen in our grief and shock. Normal relationships and casual conversations do not interest us. We prefer to remain cloistered in the hidden recesses of our own minds. A few of us mature into that suffering and come out of it with a depth that graces the rest of our lives. Others remain removed from their emotions, bitter and depressed, unwilling to give life another chance.

As a hospice social worker I worked with Alice, a woman in her mid-sixties who had lost her husband to cancer while she was in the hospital being diagnosed with end-stage lymphoma. When I met Alice she had very little time remaining. She had backed so far away from life she was almost unreachable. She seemed to have found a safe corner in a caved area of her consciousness. After listening to Alice's story I asked if there was anything that still gave her life meaning. She said there were two reasons why she still wanted to live: the love she had for her daughter and for her religion. I said that although no one would have ever wished this situation on her, I could see that her tragedies had taken her to a rich and deep purpose for living. Life for Alice was about love and spiritual growth. These losses had taken her to a depth she had not touched in health. Her pain had dropped her to a level of insight that few of us encounter.

When our backs are against the wall and we have seen our hopes eroded by loss and change, what once held our attention now seems cold and uninteresting. Our future seems uncertain or without vitality. We cannot lose ourselves in tomorrow because tomorrow holds no promise. This intense fear drops us to the base level of existence. We stand naked before life, unable to protect ourselves from the truth that has always been.

This can be a realm of penetrating insight and wisdom, or it can be a place for intense self-pity. If we learn from our pain, it can propel us into a completely different view of life's purpose. Our friends and job may change. Often our preoccupation with money and status diminishes. We lose all interest in the superficial. Our time seems more precious but without frenetic involvement. We come back fundamentally altered.

Reflecting on our death keeps us current. It allows proper prioritization of what is really important. Small things are not treated with more significance than their worth. Our perspectives shift, and there is less confusion over details and greater utilization of our energy. A growing serenity begins to take root in all aspects of our experience because we see with more clarity and depth.

Death forces us to the edge of our understanding, an edge that frightens us because of what we imagine it contains. But the secrets of life are revealed from that chasm. Much of our activity has been to ignore or escape from that view. We think that by running from the abyss we will be able to live happily ever after. We can only imagine a world containing death to be one of desolation and emptiness. This image is created from our fear, not from reality. By exploring and reflecting on death we begin to understand that loving life includes much more than we first thought. Loving life means embracing all the emotions and feelings we have about it. This includes the emotion of fear. Our fear, then, cannot distort love but actually fulfills it.

In another conversation between Carlos Castaneda and his teacher, Don Juan says: "Death is our eternal companion. . . . It has always been watching you. It always will until the day it taps you. . . . The thing to do when you're impatient is to turn to your left and ask advice from your death. An immense amount of pettiness is dropped if your death makes a gesture to you. . . . The issue of our death [is] never pressed far enough. Death is the only wise advisor that we have. Whenever you feel . . . that everything is going wrong . . . your death will tell you that you're wrong; that nothing matters outside its touch. Your death will tell you, 'I haven't touched you yet.'"

Reminding ourselves of our death keeps us in touch with the actual and allows a growing appreciation of the moment at hand. It prompts us to pay attention and remain oriented to what is true. What is forever true is this unfathomable moment in its mystery. All we have is this moment to live. It is all we will ever need. When we contact it, we rediscover the miraculous. Our heart is stirred by life as it was when we were young. Each moment contains the mystery of a lifetime. We are given the choice of exploring this moment either with openness and a willingness to learn or with an attitude that stifles creativity and perpetuates routine. The choice is continually at hand.

Observing Resistance

Reflect for a moment on a time when you were close to dying, either through an accident or a severe illness. How ready were you to die? In what ways were you not ready? What was there left to do? If you were to die today would those issues still be unresolved? What keeps you from accepting the possibility of your death in this moment? What keeps you from doing what needs to be done?

Look for opportunities to approach the subject of death and dying every day. Read the obituaries in the newspaper, visit a friend or acquaintance who is ill or dying, stop by a nursing home, read books and articles on the subject, or volunteer at a local hospice or at a critical care or oncology unit in a hospital. Observe closely how you avoid the subject of dying, and commit to learning as much as possible about it.

Reflect on your avoidance of death and dying. Would you prefer life without death? Reflect on the value and limitation of avoiding what is true. What is the relationship between circumventing reality and your suffering? What qualities of mind are you strengthening and what qualities are you neglecting when you avoid what is true?

Pick a task that you avoid or procrastinate doing, like washing the dishes or emptying the garbage. What complications arise from that avoidance? When you find you are evading some unpleasant action, look at the motivation and emotion you have associated with it. Is there fear? Are you strong enough to go ahead and do it rather than hope it will go away? See how you seek escape in your wishful thoughts (maybe someone else will do the dishes).

3 | Risking Our Lives

Does not the history of the world show that there would have been no romance in life if there had been no risks?
—MAHATMA GANDHI

AS WE GROW OLDER many of us look around and can no longer perceive mystery. We also notice we have more anxiety and insecurity. We seem to have learned to fear life rather than delight in its wonder. We may search our memory for the moment when we lost that innocence, but it was a gradual loss, almost imperceptible. As we began to focus on becoming someone in the world, something else was pushed to the background. In its place grew a sense of isolation and loneliness. There is a vague recollection of having lost something, but we have no idea how to recover it.

Working with the dying teaches us how we want to live. We have before us the life histories of the people we serve. Each dying patient is a complete book in which we are privileged to be present for the concluding chapter. A great deal can be known about the entire book from observing how that patient dies. As Elisabeth Kübler-Ross says, "People die in character." A person's attitude about his or her death and the degree of affection shown by the family and friends who have gathered are often the summation of all the pages that preceded that moment. The ending has its own momentum and direction, moving inexorably toward a conclusion based on the person's past actions.

We die the way we live. All the moments we spend enclosed within our self-righteousness, blocked to new information, reactive and opinionated, directly influence the moment of our death. So too do all the moments in which we are kind, sensitive, open, and caring. Everything we do now has a direct influence on all the future moments of our life, including our death.

As a hospice social worker I once worked with two patients, one of whom was very wealthy, the other very poor. Dorothy, the wealthy patient, lived in a multimillion-dollar mansion with numerous servants, maids, and butlers. When Dorothy became confined to a bed she placed herself in the foyer of her home so that she could remain in control. The image that is etched in my mind is Dorothy lifting her wilting arm and directing orders to her maid. With her loss of strength Dorothy became increasingly annoyed and frustrated as she was forced to face her powerlessness. Even when she was in a coma those around her would hesitate to enter the room, fearing that she would awaken and issue another order. Those who attended Dorothy seemed to respect her, but I could not discern a great deal of caring or warmth. Family members were meticulous in their attendance but evinced a coldness of heart that I found emotionally unsatisfying.

Across town in one of the harshest and most violent neighborhoods lived Roxanne, a rotund and delightful woman. She too was approaching death. I remember a large hole in the middle of her living room floor where chickens from under her house would fly in and out of her home. Roxanne would chase them away with a broom when she had the strength. I recall looking forward to visiting Roxanne. She radiated such confidence, humor, and warmth. Her acceptance of the dying process was extraordinary. I always felt refreshed after leaving her home, as if she had given me something beyond the content of the visit.

I found myself wanting to learn from Roxanne even though I was the professional caregiver. Roxanne knew something about dying that I did not know. After several weeks of visits I asked her how she had resolved her dying and could remain so quiet and peaceful. Roxanne looked at me with a serene and ageless expression and said, "Death don't scare me no more, honey. I had two of my children die in my arms. I have looked death right in the eyes and his eyes are kind."

Which of these two lives would we prefer to have lived? One woman, possessive and grasping, found she could not control her dying and maintained a bitter struggle with death. The other woman, dragged through the pain of losing her two children and imprisoned in poverty, learned from her suffering to open her heart and accept her own ending.

It becomes clear through stories such as these that each moment is precious not only for itself but also for how it prepares us for the next. Our habits harden our character, habits that may or may not allow for an easy death. Suddenly we start to die and we find ourselves fixed within a temperament that was befitting for our career but ill suited for dying. It helps to live with the end in sight. Once we understand the direction we need to travel, the greater question is, Are we willing to change?

THE URGENCY TO CHANGE

When someone dies in Thailand, the body is cremated and the ashes placed in an urn. Then, in a funeral ceremony, Buddhist monks tie a ball of string to the urn and then unwind it. By touching the string, each person attending the ceremony is directly connected to the remains. The monks then chant a verse in Pali that can be translated as: "All things are impermanent, with the nature to arise and pass away. One who lives in this truth achieves harmony and happiness with all that is."

Change is a fundamental law of existence. All around us are reminders of that truth: the changing seasons, the rising and setting of the sun, the advance and retreat of the tides, and the birth, growth, and death of plants and animals. We also have constant internal reminders: our changing moods, ideas, and interests, our precarious physical health, our aging bodies and changing abilities. But despite all these constant internal and external examples, change remains one of the most ignored facts of our time.

The law of impermanence, which accounts for our aging and eventually our death, operates in all areas of the universe. It is responsible for the creation and destruction of galaxies and solar systems. It cannot be avoided as long as we are alive. For a short time the elements that make up the body are in balance, and we say we are healthy and alive. As long as our good health continues, many of us forget about impermanence; we take our health for granted and expect it as our birthright. But soon the law makes itself known, and we notice ourselves aging. We have pain where there has never been pain before, and our memory is not as dependable. The principle has always been acting within us, but until now we have chosen to ignore it.

We often operate as if we live outside the influence of this law, as if this truth applies to everything except ourselves. We are shocked when we feel its weight in our lives: when our new car becomes scratched, when our child grows up and leaves home, when someone close to us dies, or when we become terminally ill. One eighty-seven-year-old patient on our hospice service protested her illness with the vehemence of youth, as if she were twenty and being robbed of a complete life. Death always comes too soon when we live outside the law of impermanence.

How can we expect to grow as a human being if we envision ourselves as living outside the law of change? The passion and urgency to change comes when we have learned we are part of this law, when we have integrated impermanence into our behavior and our being. We grow when we allow ourselves to be altered. Growth becomes a natural byproduct when we atune to change.

We may resist reality's perpetual motion, but eventually our resistances to change weaken if we rub against it long enough. Change becomes impossible to ignore when we reflect upon our aging process and eventual death. We become ready to risk letting go of our holding patterns because we see clearly that the alternative to movement is stagnation and that stagnation is suffering.

Whenever we attempt to arrest the natural evolution of one state into the next, we attempt to freeze the unfreezable. In doing so it is we that stagnate, not life. Resisting change, the Buddha said, is like holding on to the wheel of a moving oxcart. Sooner or later we get run over. All of our manipulation does nothing to alter the course of events. It merely causes us to be unprepared when those events do occur.

Our choices are clearly before us at all times. We can pretend we do not age and die; but this will lead to multiple problems and difficulties. Or we can live in accordance with the way things are. Early on, we begin to either defend ourselves against change or develop an attitude that accommodates it. Over time we either become cynical and fearful in respect to transitions or see change as an opportunity and a potential for the birth of something new. Those who choose a defensive stance begin to protect themselves, their families, their possessions. They experience an ever greater anxiety about loss and a growing reluctance to share. Those who accept change start to emphasize personal and familial growth. They work positively with new situations as they arise, and they are eager to learn and try new things.

We can often see the beginning of these two different psychic postures in the play of small children. One child will be exploring the world with enthusiasm, less concerned about soiling her clothes than about the excitement of the investigation. The other child will hold herself back from play to be proper and protect her cleanliness. Both styles have their advantages, and neither style is the right way to be at all times. What we want to watch is whether these tendencies harden into lifetime patterns that reduce the person's ability to adapt to new situations.

Growth does not limit itself to defending what has been accomplished in the past but looks toward the future for expansion. For growth to occur we have to be willing to let go of long-established habit patterns; only then can we allow ourselves to be pulled in a new direction. If we construct our lives solely to maintain our security, we remain hesitant and bound by fear. We can stay on the edge of our growth only when we are willing to risk facing our fear.

This is not to imply that change is always a better choice than the status quo. Sometimes the wisest thing to do is to stay the course and be consistent. It is not the choice itself that is the problem but the attitude from which we choose. When we act wisely we do something because it needs to be done, not because we are afraid of the alternative. Either we remain insulated and afraid, or we risk. Resisting change moves us in opposition to the natural flow of events. Our creativity and spontaneity wither.

Whereas growth implies moving beyond our self-imposed limitations, fear keeps us imprisoned in habits and routines. Fear keeps us caged behind our perceived order. It confines us to the known and expected even as our heart yearns for greater expansiveness. Remembering our death can allow us to access the courage to risk doing something challenging and new. When we forget our death we frequently forgo our growth for the safety of perceived permanence.

My friend Art, a meditation teacher, is HIV positive. His health is precarious at best, and when I am with him I never know whether it will be the last time I will see him alive. He speaks publicly about his illness. Because I have worked in hospice for a number of years we occasionally team up to present death-and-dying workshops. I always come away from these workshops feeling invigorated by Art's focus and the energy he devotes to growth. When I ask him what gives him such single-minded resolve, he responds, "My illness." Art is on his edge and clearly sees growth as the single purpose of his life. I am safe with my health and often compromise growth because I think I have time to delay. Even though I work with the dying on a daily basis, it often takes this very ill friend of mine to wake me up and show me that I am resting in safety.

Change comes whether we want it or not. The question is, How much pain and fear will we allow ourselves to go through before we accept the inevitable? Change is threatening because we have no way of knowing how we will be altered when we surrender to growth. When we go against our habit patterns to accommodate change, we risk changing into someone different, and this may frighten us. So we will resist growth until we are sufficiently fed up with our lethargy. As our last and final choice, only after we understand we have no other, we will reluctantly plunge into growth. Most of us never reach this point. Sadly, we never manage the next step, where we cross the abyss of our fear and fall into the realm of our heart.

Acknowledging the law of impermanence will force our heart to risk confronting our fear. Risk lies at the boundary between fear and growth. It is action taken without certainty to free ourselves from dullness. We do not know what will happen, but we know that the alternative—staying the same—proves intolerable. The truly remarkable thing is not that we become dull but that we stay in that dullness until we die. It is remarkable because we know what we are doing yet are still afraid to risk.

Life responds when we risk. It meets us more than halfway and almost always demonstrates that the risk was worth taking. The heart's sure release is in moving with that risk. It is in taking that step without assurances. Do we want to be seventy years old and saying to ourselves on our deathbed, "I wish I had . . ."? The way to prevent this regret is to live and risk in a never-ending journey deeper into our hearts. Are we willing to die to our old ways and risk the new? With experience our faith in this uncharted path of the heart will mature, and our mind will give up its battle for control. There is no other way to open the door to our heart except by risking our fears. What do we have to lose?

FROM FEAR TO AFFECTION

Physical death is a more dramatic manifestation of the dying that goes on continually throughout the day. We are perpetually facing the beginning and endings of situations and circumstances without appreciating the emotional toll that these small births and deaths have on our lives. Change itself is a death. It can be as subtle as forgetting a thought or as common as falling asleep. Every death impacts our consciousness when we resist the transition. Resisting is an attempt to maintain continuity and is thus a denial of the new. Every death leads us into the fear of a new reality and leaves the grief of the old in its wake.

What makes physical death so poignant is its absoluteness. With physical death there will be no more human relationships, no more sensory enjoyment, no more touching the earth. The dying give up everything they have ever known. When the mind faces the enormity of that loss tremendous fear can arise.

Once during a three-month mindfulness retreat I was made aware of the power of this fear. Mindfulness practice attempts to focus our attention on our mind and body experiences by allowing these experiences to occur without distortion or judgment. During an early morning sitting I suddenly felt my body begin to die. I knew it was not this body that was dying. Perhaps it was a long-lost memory of a death in some other time, but all the sensations were being felt in the present. I remember my heart feeling crushed in my chest and my breath becoming labored. The pain was excruciating. I was having a heart attack and knew the body was dying. What I remember the most about this process was the immense fear that accompanied it. The fear felt primal, almost cellular, it was so basic to survival. The moment after I died I had the thought, "My God, I was not aware." The fear had been too strong for any continuity of attention during my death. This was the first indication I had of the power of the fear of dissolution.

In one of the Buddhist discourses a Brahman asked the Buddha if all mortals fear dying. The Buddha responded that not all people are afraid to die. He said, "Only those who thirst after sense pleasure, or thirst after the body, or perform a lifetime of unwholesome deeds, or are confused about the way things are, fear death." That probably covers most of us. How we handle the daily deaths associated with loss and change tells us a great deal about the problems we will face when we physically die.

Precisely because death represents such absoluteness, such total and complete abandonment to the unknown, it is at the same time a crucial moment for our growth and understanding. Physical death is the ultimate edge for learning and growth because of the magnitude of the risk associated with it. The risk is unequivocal. There is no choice, no turning back, and no compromise.

Any death, physical or otherwise, is an edge between what we know and what we do not. It is the boundary between security and insecurity, between certainty and uncertainty, between reality as we know it and the mystery of the unknown. We resist the mystery because we translate the mysterious into the fearful. Our fears say, "I will be in torment. There is nothing beyond this life. Death is extinction." But what we are actually doing is projecting our fears onto the unknown and then living them out as if the unknown moment were the known. We need to look directly at what our fear says will happen in death in order to open death to other possibilities.

Fear predicts an imaginary reality. It masks what is actually happening with our concerns for what might occur. If we can go through what we fear will happen, the real truth of the experience will unfold. The mystery of the moment will be revealed. A few years ago I saw a television commercial for camera film. The ad opened by panning the New York City skyline at night. Viewers believe they are seeing the city, until an airplane bursts through the image and they understand that what they thought was the city was only a photograph—an illusion. Fear is like that photograph, illusory and paper-thin.

We project the certainty of our convictions onto an experience only to have a very different situation unfold. At the outset we do not know whether reality will correspond to our projection. So we must have passion for the unknown in order to penetrate our fear. With passion we are willing to take risks and test the reality of our fear.

To move through fear we need to convince ourselves that it is worth doing. Strategies like evasion and denial never work for very long and create more suffering than we imagine. Opening to the unknown fear cannot be any worse than what we go through to protect ourselves from it. Reality just keeps coming at us until our resistances are dropped, and we have no other choice but to surrender to our worst-case scenario. Most people would rather stay in the fires of a known hell than risk shattering their world view and leap into the fireman's net. But when we are dying our world is irretrievable. At that point it makes sense to open to the dying process because everything we know will soon be lost, no matter what we do. Since we have no other choice but to go along for the ride, we might as well do it as openly as we can.

With a little more scrutiny we realize that our safe world was never really safe at all. We have always been living with the unknown but have refused to call it by name. When we understand that both life and death are journeys from an unknowable moment into an unknown future, we realize that both provide the same potential to grow. The difference between the two narrows.

People who are dying occasionally sense this. As a hospice social worker I worked with Donna, a middle-aged mother of four. Until her prognosis was irreversible she struggled desperately to maintain a semblance of normalcy with her family. But as the time of her death grew unavoidably closer, Donna asked that the pictures of her family and reminders of her life be taken away from her bedside. She said it was time to move into the mysterious world of the beyond, and she wanted nothing to hold her back. She told her family she loved them and then began to redirect her focus. The family understood her wishes and replaced their photos with pictures of Christ. Donna would stare for hours at the pictures. She seemed to die moving effortlessly from the certainty of what she knew into the mystery of where she was going.

Donna's growing serenity testified to her ability to let go of fear and surrender into an undefined moment. She was unusual in her willingness to step away from the security she had always known and move into incertitude. After her death Donna's family remarked on her contentment, acceptance, and quiet wisdom during those last days.

Fear is found wherever we hold ourselves back from a full participation in life. The greater the fear, the more the resistance. Once we overcome our resistance and step through fear, however, we find ourselves immersed in the unknown. The more fear a situation contains, the greater the potential for wisdom. Growth occurs when we pass through our fear. In moving through death, our fear transforms into an appreciation of the process itself. The heart moves into an affection for all things. In resistance, the heart is a fortress; the walls come up, and we lose our ability to be intimate. In affection, the heart is like an open field; we can reach beyond our individual concerns and intimately touch another person.

I learned this lesson from Anna, a nine-year-old girl who was dying from cystic fibrosis. I was the hospice social worker. Her mother had recently sought a separation from her father, and her father was in a great deal of pain over both this and Anna's illness. We were all gathered at Anna's bed during a breathing crisis in which the child was craning her neck to force as much air as possible into her lungs. After exerting a great deal of uncomfortable effort, Anna looked up and waved us out of the room. Being the social worker, I tried to prepare the family for the fact that Anna was probably ready to die and wanted to be left alone. What she was actually doing behind the closed door was struggling out of bed to reach the table. There at the table she made a big "I love you" poster for her father. Anna called us all back into the room and gave the poster to him. She died about a week later. Her father had the poster framed.

When I think of affection, Anna comes to mind. This little girl was able to free herself from her own fear and reach out to another in pain. Death and dying can bring a maturity and understanding beyond one's chronological age. Within this small and frail body was a mind that was acutely alert and sensitive to the needs of others. Anna was both focused on her breathing and keenly aware of the broader picture. This little girl had no time "to be dying" in the sense of dwelling on her own demise. Seeing her father's pain, she wanted him to feel better. Affection has the wonderful characteristic of not taking sides. Anna was not angry at her mother for leaving her father, but her heart had opened to her father's suffering, and she acted accordingly. Affection does what is appropriate without looking for reward.

Each of us has within our being the ability to love and to fear. Our heart settles into love when the mind runs out of options. When we are dying there are no choices left. We may project our fears from life onto our death, but life as we know it is near its end. Fearing death is the final futile attempt of the mind to hold us back. There is nothing we can do except move ahead. When we move through our fears, acknowledging them without resistance, our fears vanish into the emptiness from which they came. What are left are an affectionate heart and an alert, sensitive mind.

Habits and Change

Reflect on the impermanence of life. Everything that is born will eventually die. Is there anything that falls outside this law? Think about the things that make you happy: your family and friends, your job and income, your hobbies—the list goes on. Reflect on everything that has contributed to your happiness, now and in the past. How much time do you spend attending to them? How much do you depend on them for your stability and security? Look ahead several years. How many of these sources of happiness are still around? How many will be there with you on your deathbed? Is there lasting happiness from any of them? Consider the relationship between happiness and change. Are they as diametrically opposed as they seem?

Find a quiet place, close your eyes, and spend ten minutes each day listening to the changing sounds around you. Notice the alterations of pitches, sounds, and tones. After you have been listening for a while, choose another sense to observe, perhaps sight. Go outdoors and watch nature very carefully. Notice the movement and flux within your visual field. Actually see that life is motion. Continue on with similar studies of each of the five senses, observing the subtle changes and movements that each sense perceives. Spend some time observing your inner world of thoughts and emotions. Does the law of impermanence also affect these? Watch your emotions during the course of a day. What happens with the intensity and duration of these states of mind? What can you conclude about their relationship to change?

Reflect on a time when you took a significant risk. What was it like to live in that way? Was there fear or excitement? Did it turn out all right? Now reflect on your current life. Where do you seek safety and security? Are you content with your life as it is? Are you the person you want to be? Are you doing what you want to do? At what expense do you maintain your current lifestyle? What avenues are open to you for initiating change? Sit quietly and reflect on the times when you hold yourself back, when your heart is pulling you toward change and you refuse to risk. What are you afraid will happen if you risk changing?

Choose a small challenge, something that seems achievable, which you feel your heart is calling you to do. An example might be asking for a raise or telling your neighbor about some annoyance that he or she causes you. Notice the fear in even considering the action. Just feel the fear and watch how it controls your thoughts. Can you risk what the fear tells you might happen? Thinking about risking is not enough; it requires follow-through. Challenge yourself to learn to risk, and then go ahead and act. Feel your heart's joy when you are released from the fear.

Reflect on your habits. Do you bite your nails, for example, or have other nervous habits? Such habits are your safety zones, where you do not have to think about new ways of being. Some seem necessary, others do not. Which of your habits are more of a hindrance in your life than help? Think about why you continue to act in certain habitual ways. Is there creativity and spontaneity in your habit patterns? Is fear related to these patterns?

Study one of your habit patterns for several days. Let it teach you, without interfering with it in any way. Feel how it serves you, how easy it is to act within a known pattern. Try to become aware of yourself in the midst of the habitual activity. Use the habit as a cue to wake yourself up. Notice the effect of your awareness on the habit itself. Does the awareness free you from the routine of habitual response? Is there a relationship between this awareness and spontaneity?

Reflect on the Buddha's response when he was asked, "Do all mortals fear dying?" He is reported to have said: "Only those who thirst after sense pleasure, or thirst after the body, or perform a lifetime of unwholesome deeds, or are confused about the way things are, fear death." Reflect on how involved you are in the pursuit of sense pleasures, how much you are driven by sexual impulses, how often you find yourself acting unskillfully, and how much confusion you experience in your life.

Pick one of the Buddha's categories that best exemplifies you. Study this pattern in yourself all week long. Watch every facet of how it operates. (Above all, be easy with yourself. This is not an exercise to reinforce self-hatred!) How does this pattern keep you resisting any thoughts of your death? Can you visualize yourself on your deathbed and sense how this pattern might hold you back from letting go into the unknown? Conversely, can you see how reflecting on death might help you with this pattern?

4 | Acknowledging the Shadow

Behind the repressed darkness and the personal shadow—
that which has been and is rotting and that which is not
yet and is germinating—is the archetypal darkness,
the principle of not-being, which has been named the Devil,
as Evil, as Original Sin, as Death, as Nothingness.
—JAMES HILLMAN

WHILE WE ARE DYING we may not have the strength to
hold our psychic defenses in place. The parts of ourselves that we have
long avoided and feared often return. Waiting in the darkened recesses
of our consciousness lays the shadow, the forbidden side of our character, created by our fears and resistances. The shadow expresses itself
through such mental habits as impatience, low self-esteem, hatred, and
lust. It is here that dying takes us; it is here that we can soften and open
to our whole being.

A shadow is cast only where light is obstructed. The shadow within
our consciousness is created when the light of our self-acceptance is
smothered by self-criticism, abnegation, and dislike. Our delight with
one aspect of ourselves defines in the same moment our disgust for the
shadowed opposite part. Fear of our shadow has kept us from acknowledging it as part of ourselves. Subconsciously we have screened our
mental responses, permitting access to the ones that we like and disas-
sociating from the others. The result of employing our defenses against
the shadow is a growing conflict between our ideal self-image and the
reality of who we are. Aversion creates a tension that forces the shadow
to the surface even as we despise its appearance.

The mind contains all possibilities. The entire continuum of mental
states can manifest within us because the range of the mind is all-
encompassing. Under the right conditions we are vulnerable to any

given emotion or attitude. We can temporarily repress certain states of mind, but over time those same attributes will return in force. We attempt to hold these qualities at bay through a variety of defense mechanisms, but we eventually end up dealing with their energies in one way or another.

The emergence of the shadow suggests that our mental lives are not entirely under our conscious control. The shadow responds to our aversion by becoming more dominant, not less. Nothing can be eliminated from the mind by willful intentions. We can hide from these qualities and pretend they do not exist or suppress them in our unconscious, but their power and force are only multiplied by our inattention. The effect of this is that the more life is lived under the influence of the shadow, the more we attempt to discard it from our view.

Fracturing our mental lives—our thoughts, attitudes, and beliefs—into the good and the bad is the work of the shadow. This inward activity simultaneously leads toward external divisions as well. Life and death are polar opposites that form in the wake of the shadow's activity. Life is seen as the force of good, light, creation, and love, while death is cloaked in destruction, evil, and desolation. Having created this imaginary division, we pit one against the other. We fracture the original wholeness of life by demanding it to be only one way. The division is entirely mind-created. It is the splitting off of what we want from what we resist. Our conflict is internal not external. We struggle with our fears and desires and project the resulting confusion onto the natural unity inherent in life.

Carl Jung once remarked that he would rather be whole than good. Perhaps he meant that when we attempt to be good we paradoxically force the emergence of evil within ourselves, but when we allow the coexistence of good and bad within our psyche, out of that wholeness goodness will naturally manifest. We think that if we do not keep a constant check on ourselves, we might become the tyrant that we most fear. However, it is the checking itself that divides the world and leads to tyranny. Before our checking there is natural harmony and symmetry; afterwards, however, the world becomes contentious and antagonistic. Our own mind creates this duality.

SEPARATING LIFE AND DEATH

One of the great divisions created from our shadow is the disjoining of life from death. Often dying patients do not acknowledge this separation and talk about "returning home." This is the beginning of unifying the two halves. Most of us find it difficult to rest comfortably with thoughts of death in the middle of good health. We see existence as the opposite of extinction. We then pit our existence against our extinction in a contest we are bound to lose.

The world is awash in images of this contest, this separation of life from death. We portray death as the robber of life, a phantom cloaked in black that waits in darkness to descend upon its victim. We would like nothing better than to sweep the streets clean of all suggestions of our mortality. Many doctors view death as a failure of their profession, as if we were meant to live forever. The status of physicians in a society indicates its aversion to death and dying. We elevate the rank of those who, we feel, protect us against the thing we most fear.

One of the reasons death is viewed as inimical to life is because it causes pain. Virtually everyone at some point suffers the loss of a loved one, and the grief that follows is one of the most difficult emotions to endure because it can rob us of our purpose to live. It leaves us feeling as if life is devoid of meaning. If everything is taken away in death, what sense does life make?

Death eliminates everything we now see. A person dies and the life force is gone with only a shell remaining. Death revokes life, removes it from view, and therefore stands in opposition to it. It is difficult to see life in any other way except through the presence or absence of its forms. There is happiness when life is here and pain when it is gone. Life is valuable, death is not. Everything of value stands in contrast to its absence.

Many religions teach that life and death are two forms of the same truth. This was one of the messages of Christ when he died on Friday and was resurrected on Sunday. Why did he wait two days before reappearing to the world? Surely he could have arisen from the dead immediately if he had wanted to. During that time there was an enormous outpouring of grief from his followers. His return demonstrated that their grief had been misplaced. He allowed his followers to dwell in their misrepresentation of death, hoping that their pain would eventually open them to the truth of who he was. The act of grieving over his body was a denial that he lived outside of the corporal form.

Separating what we can see from what we cannot is the first step in creating the shadow. What we see is familiar to us. We rest comfortably where we feel safe. What we cannot see is unknown and usually feared. We hold tightly to life because we are afraid of its absence, which we project as annihilation, the void, and nothingness. We think of nothingness as a desert or as the vacuum of space. The end of life terrorizes us, so we shove it out of view, away from our conscious awareness, and let it assume the form of the shadow.

But by pretending death does not exist, we have not eliminated it; we have only closed our eyes. Its presence is still felt in our reactions. Our fear and anger are an indication of the presence of the shadow. When we react we know that the shadow is behind the activity, and one of our strongly held beliefs, attitudes, or self-images is being threatened. Fear and the need to protect our self-image lead to emotional outbursts, eruptions that happen so quickly that we never understand what led to them.

We fight the intrusion of the shadow by holding fast to who we want to be. The shadow contains what we fear we might become. We shove what we fear down below the level of our awareness into the unconscious and then attempt to live out only desired qualities. The unconscious, which contains the shadow, is not a separately sealed section of our minds. It is just that fear has eclipsed it from view.

The language of the unconscious can be confusing to our intellect. The imagery and intense emotions are fearful. Some of its messages seem to pertain to the life we are living, and others seem more rooted in our collective humanity. Our rational minds like ideas in nicely bundled thoughts that make historic sense. The rational mind and the unconscious are like two people who attempt to communicate but speak different languages. To the dominant rational mind the unconscious is neither predictable nor consistent. Its presence seems mysterious and dangerous. The emotional charge of its language can easily throw us off center.

The unconscious threatens us only because we misunderstand it. If we allow it to speak its own language without censuring it, we can begin to hear what it says. To understand the shadow without distorting it, however, we need to let go of the fear that surrounds it. Although we may not be able to understand it using our intellect, we can begin to feel its expression and open to its rich imagery. Then it will tell us its story. That story may be disturbing or confusing, but it is our story and part of ourselves.

I worked with Ellis, a hospice patient, who had a recurring nightmare about death. He tried everything to keep from having the dream, but night after night he found himself alone in a room with a dark and mysterious shadowy spirit. When the apparition would begin to approach him, he would run away in terror. He could feel the figure's intense stare even as he ran, and then he would wake up in a panic. The following night he would have the dream again. As we worked together over several weeks I suggested he personalize death by giving it a name and asking it questions. We role-played the parts several times. He began to read accounts about dying and developed a genuine curiosity and interest in what death was like. One night as the same dream unfolded, he stopped running and turned around to meet death. He said his interest in death in that moment was stronger than his fear. As he turned toward death it vanished, and he never had the recurring nightmare again.

Ellis was able to develop interest in the thing he feared the most. When he gave death his attention, he began to allow it as part of his consciousness, and its horror diminished in the light of his understanding. Even after the dream disappeared, Ellis had to renew his commitment to face his shadow. But the success he had in befriending his death convinced him that he could work with his difficulties.

But the shadow is a shadow only because of the power we give it. In the final evaluation neither the shadow nor its offspring, death, has ever been the problem. It is our aversion to what we think the shadow says about us that creates our desire to escape its message. Resisting death, we hold tightly to life. Our endless striving to avoid the shadow leads us to react to both living and dying. We desire the one and fear the other, thereby creating an inherent tension in which there is neither enjoyment of life nor understanding of death. Holding death at arm's length, we end up resisting life to the same degree.

THE MEETING OF LIFE AND DEATH

Many patients who are dying no longer belong to a world that is fractured into life and death. When we know we are approaching the end of our lives we can no longer sustain our usual denial of death. Hospice patients who have this knowledge realize it is time to withdraw their energy and focus from the living. Sometimes there is a period of withdrawal in which patients will turn away from social interaction and move deeply into themselves. They will frequently come out of that period more remote and removed from family and friends. Their whole view may have shifted so that they now seem to live between two worlds rather than fixed exclusively in this one. Sometimes a patient will look through the person in front of him and attempt to communicate with people who cannot be seen. He will often gaze past this world and rest upon something or someone distant and hidden. It should be noted that these visions are not frightening to the patient. In fact the opposite is true; they seem to offer the patient reassurance and comfort.

Medically, these perceptions are caused by a decrease in the circulation of oxygen to the brain and a change in the body's metabolism. But this physical explanation is only a partial one. For anyone who has seen a person go through these reality shifts, it is clear that this other world is as real to him as this one is to us. He is not hallucinating. We cannot dismiss what we witness with a medical banality merely because we cannot reference those same perceptions.

More to the point, the patient's view becomes more holistic when she no longer divides life and death into separate camps but indeed experiences them as a seamless continuum. When the patient frees herself from that false division, she may gain access to unseen worlds, worlds that would be available to all of us were we not so intent on fracturing this one.

Margaret was an elderly woman dying of breast cancer. When hospice first became involved, Margaret claimed that death was the absolute end and nothing existed beyond it. As she became more confined to her bed, Margaret would spend increasingly long periods by herself. Normally she was an extroverted woman, and her sudden desire for isolation concerned her family. As she became weaker she started to go in and out of a coma. The family noticed she would move her lips in silent speech to unseen people while she was in a semicomatose state. Once the hospice nurse gently called her name while she was in one of these states. "Margaret, Margaret, can you hear me?" The patient, focusing on something beyond what the nurse could see, looked through her and replied, "Margaret is not here right now. Her friends have come to take her away. She'll be back soon." A few minutes later her eyes were clear, and she spoke to the nurse about "going home." Two hours later she died very peacefully.

The question is how do we face our shadow? Do we divide the whole into opposing parts, creating a multitude of problems including the struggle between life and death? If we were able to discard part of our minds the solution would be simple. We could get rid of the shadow and live happily ever after. But obviously there is no way to eliminate any part of our consciousness. Even to think that the shadow could be extracted from the rest of the mind implies a misconception about its origin. The shadow exists only because we want life on our own terms and are unwilling to accept it as it is.

We see this in our ideas of good and evil and the suffering created from this division. If we look closely, we will see that evil is built upon our need to guard against further pain. When we suffer we pull back, separate, and protect ourselves against any intrusion. Hostility, rage, selfishness, dishonesty, and most other "negative" qualities are the result of insulating ourselves from our hearts. We think the way to heal is to keep everything at bay as if we needed fortification from further attacks. It becomes the world against us. It is light against dark. We become our own worst enemy.

As we learn from reflecting on death, we can use a different strategy to reclaim our nature and begin to heal. This lesson is not limited to the dying; the message is equally appropriate to the healthy. The reconciliation needed is for both sides of our character to coexist within the whole of our consciousness. Like the dying patient who heals himself by no longer warring against death, we also need to stop living a struggle we have created with our imagination. We end our suffering when we understand that we are diminished as human beings when any part of our character is denied. It is not a matter of being good or bad but of being complete and total. We have it all, why not be it all? Anything less forces the shadow to rule from behind the scenes.

The tapestry of existence is woven of many strands. Our character expresses the entire range of mental qualities manifesting in each moment. We are only what we are right now: no more, no less. No other side of our character lurks in the background waiting for an opportunity to take control, because that other side is part of our life in this moment as well. Everything can be dealt with here and now. Being whole means honoring all of these manifestations in the present. Once this is done, the energy that we put into maintaining our separation becomes available for more creative endeavors. Life and death return to their original unification.

Kendall was a hospice patient who was at war with his own history. He had mentally and physically abused his wife and daughter throughout much of their life together. Kendall had been an alcoholic for forty years. On the suggestion of his doctor in order to avoid further complications, he was still given alcohol throughout his illness. As he began to deal with his dying, his family could frequently hear him sobbing alone in his room. He hated the person he had become and lived with an enormous guilt and fear of his temper and rage. Kendall spent long sessions with the hospice chaplain seeking self-forgiveness and praying for forgiveness from God. Even in the midst of this self-degradation he would still fall into a hostile rage if his family made a simple mistake in his care. These outbursts would eventually propel him into further self-torment.

Unexpectedly, Kendall suddenly fell into a deep coma. Everyone thought he was dying and made all the necessary arrangements. Three days later he woke up and was completely alert and responsive. After a short period of time everyone who knew him realized something had changed. The anger had disappeared, and he seemed more relaxed and less self-deprecating. When the chaplain asked him about these differences, he said he was tired of hating himself. He said he had to pull all parts of himself together to face his dying.

To paraphrase Abraham Lincoln, "A mind divided against itself cannot stand." Kendall understood he had enough difficulty facing his death without the additional burden of self-hatred. Who knows what happened to him while he was in a coma? The point is that he came out of this reverie with a strong sense of personal integration and a diminished shadow.

Dying teaches us that we will not be engulfed by evil if we permit the dark side to share time and space with the good. We see contentment expressed by many of those near death. Their message is that basic goodness lies in our wholeness, not in our struggle against evil. The goodness that manifests from the absence of conflict has no opposite. When something contains everything there can be no force aligned against it. It stands without opposition, rightly integrated.

The Shadow

Reflect on the enormous range of behavior and emotion within yourself and recognize that in response to every news story you could say, "There, but for the grace of God, go I." With similar birth conditions and life circumstances, you could be the thief or the heroine, the person with AIDS or the homeless. Reflect on the range of your own emotions, on how whimsical or circumstantial they can seem. If you were provoked in the right situation, is there any activity or emotion beyond your own potential to feel, think, or do?

Bring to mind a time when people you know have been thoughtful and have acted with good intentions. Feel how easy it is to care about and open your heart to them. Now bring to mind criminals and their crimes. Watch your heart close toward the rapist, murderer, and thief and recognize that their hearts are also closed. They acted out of their own suffering and perpetuated their pain in a chain reaction that has now closed your own heart. Feel the energy you expend to keep such people out of your life. Can you begin to open to even this kind of human suffering? Can you see such people as worthy of your caring even if they are deserving of punishment?

Reflect upon the changing intensity and quality of your emotional life. Emotions are not static conditions but fluctuating states of mind. What is actually contained within an emotion such as happiness? How long does it usually last? What conditions need to be present for happiness to manifest? How much control do you actually have over your emotions?

Choose any attitude or emotion that you experience often, such as anger or sexual desire. Over the next few days, try to notice the fluctuations in intensity of this state of mind. If you choose anger, for example, become aware of your feelings of annoyance, frustration, irritability, hostility, and rage. Notice how you relate to these variations in energy and activity. When do you lose your self-awareness? Are these feelings uncomfortable? Do you identify with all aspects of the emotion or only a certain range of its intensity? Feel the most uncomfortable part of the emotion. Can you allow it to be in your consciousness without acting it out?

Reflect on Carl Jung's statement that he would rather be whole than good. What does this mean to you? Think about a time when you were self-righteous. How did that feel? Was there a feeling of separation and distance from others? If you acted out or verbalized your feeling of self-righteousness, what consequences did it have? Reflect on what it means to be whole and complete without emphasizing any quality at all.

Choose a personal quality that you are proud of, such as your kindness, humility, or courage. Select a quality that you strongly identify with and that makes a clear statement about who you are. How do you feel when this quality expresses itself in action? Now look at its opposite: your anger, arrogance, or weakness. How do you feel when this opposite quality arises? Watch the arising and passing of both of these states. Now attempt to exclude the opposite quality entirely. Watch it over time and see what happens. Can it be done? What happens to the positive quality as you try to exclude the negative? What does this tell you about the nature of the mind?

Reflect on polar opposites, seeing how one defines the other. How would you know one side existed without the other? Can you see opposites as different ends of the same continuum rather than as two separate qualities? Take any pair, such as worthiness and unworthiness, or likability and unlikability. Where would you put yourself along a continuum between the two? Reflect on the struggle to maintain your likability or self-worth when your inward life is always changing.

Choose any pair of opposites and investigate it for one week. For example, observe your tendencies toward honesty and dishonesty, generosity and selfishness, or clarity and confusion. Study both tendencies, and see how you attempt to strengthen one at the expense of the other. Keep reminding yourself of their relativity: no matter where you are on the scale, there is more to achieve. Are you ever kind or generous enough? Is there any rest or contentment when you evaluate yourself in this way? Rather than attempting to strengthen one of the opposites, bring both within you. Bring your striving into awareness as well. Be vigilant of the full range of qualities along the scale without judging yourself by the presence or absence of any quality at all. Now step off the scale and allow all measurements to end.

5 | Being Human

To be a human being ought not to require any special
considerations, special training, preparation, plans, study,
effort. It should be natural, unlabored, without thought
or consideration, spontaneous. If your activity does require
any self-conscious effort, then you are not truly, honestly,
a human being. You are only trying in that direction.
—JAE JAH NOH, *DO YOU SEE WHAT I SEE?*

ONCE WE BEGIN TO ACKNOWLEDGE the shadow, we under-
stand how our fear of it has kept us within its influence and separated us
from our spontaneity. We have spent a great deal of time trying to meet
the expectations of others and defend ourselves from hurtful criticism.
We attempt to manifest only those parts of ourselves we want others
to know. When the shadow is brought to light and seen as an inherent
part of who we are, we can drop our defenses and live the life of a full
human being. The entire range of emotions is open to us, and our hearts
become more sensitive and caring.

Everywhere we see evidence of the struggle to come to terms with
our human nature. Our bookstores are filled with information on how
to be natural. Psychotherapists and spiritual teachers instruct us how to
become whole and complete. Naturalness is the buzzword that sells soft
drinks and cosmetics. Weekly workshops offered around the country
focus on uncovering our natural abilities. We market the task of being
natural as if it were a commodity.

Almost everyone is interested in becoming more spontaneous and
creative. We set about developing these qualities as we would with any
self-development project, through hard work and perseverance. We put
ourselves through arduous spiritual disciplines and self-improvement
seminars. We allow commercials and professionals to define where that

effort will take us and then work hard to become these marketed images. By doing so we remain one step removed from what naturalness really is.

Several years ago there was an interview with a noted comedian who was famous for his vocal imitations. After several sessions, the interviewer grew frustrated with the comic because he never spoke from his own voice. Whenever he was questioned, he would fall into one of his verbal impersonations and speak like that character. Finally the interviewer requested that the comedian answer in his own voice. The man tried to find his natural speech but ended by saying he was not sure anymore which sound was his own. The interviewer noted there is something tragic about someone who does not know his own voice.

But many of us have also lost parts of our own voice. We have sometimes willfully and sometimes unknowingly allowed pieces of our personality to be isolated from our consciousness. Somewhere along the way we have learned to change ourselves to fit the expectations of others. The idea of protecting this secondhand image becomes so pervasive that we begin to lose the coordinates and ground of our being. Over time, this substitute image becomes our relationship to the world, and we are left with the emptiness of being a very different person than who we naturally are. The need we have to please other people distances us from our own voice.

Some of us believe if we ever opened the door to our humanity we would be overwhelmed by our passion, lust, rage, and fear. We think that what it means to be natural is to let ourselves go and act from these tendencies like a wild animal. We fear a loss of control and a society without order. But naturalness is not self-indulgence; it is self-honesty. It is facing all of our tendencies, learning from them, and acting from this clarity. As long as we pretend parts of ourselves do not exist, we remain under the influence of the shadow.

Our sense of unworthiness is at the heart of pretending to be other than who we are. Naturalness becomes secondary to maintaining an image that protects us from contacting our self-dislike. Because of this poor self-image we check and censure our activity. When we meet someone, we project our interpretation of her expectations onto our behavior and then criticize ourselves for not meeting the ideal standards we set.

An internal monologue ensues that assesses other people's reactions to us and judges our behavior accordingly. We never really question this image because we have such a low opinion of our character that we commit ourselves to being anyone but who we are.

The extraordinary mime Marcel Marceau performed a skit called "The Mask Maker." The skit opened with the mask maker creating smiling and frowning masks in his shop. Using no props, the mime changed his face to appear as if different masks were being tried on. After putting on and taking off several masks, a smiling mask unexpectedly became stuck on his face. He attempted in desperation to pull it off, as the audience viewed a smiling, grinning face on a body struggling with the pain of tearing the mask off. Finally the mask maker was able to rip the happy mask from his face, disclosing the wretched distress and fear under the mask.

Many of us feel the pain of covering our natural face with the pretension that society demands from us. We have somehow learned to forsake our real feelings and assume the posture that is most fitting to the circumstances. We are supposed to be happy at a party, sad and melancholy at a funeral, and serious and focused during a management meeting. Who we are, as we move in and out of various situations, gets lost in the shuffle. We sometimes find ourselves laughing when we feel like crying and despondent when there is no obvious reason to be disturbed. We have spent so much time following the dictates of people and situations we have forgotten who lies under the mask.

We want to be natural, but many of us do not want to be who we are. We have grown up with the idea that there is something intrinsically wrong with us. We believe that if we could change in a certain way, we could then become natural. But how can we possibly be natural without being who we already are? This contradiction does not seem to cause us hesitation. We spend an enormous amount of time and money on both self-improvement and polishing our image. The self that we have is seldom seen to be good enough. Our ideal self is just beyond that next therapy session and interactive workshop. The more energy we spend seeking a better personality, the less attention we give the real problem, our lack of self-acceptance.

Being human is our condition and does not require any additional development. We only need to open to who we already are. Naturalness is inherent in being alive; it is our birthright. We can ignore or hide from it, but it is always waiting to reclaim its place. Like the mask maker, we frequently have layers of pretension painted upon our natural character. These layers have been our defense against unwanted intrusion. They have not only kept others at bay, they have also made us strangers to ourselves. We have protected ourselves from what we are afraid to be. We have lived with this behavior for so long we forget what it was protecting us from.

What can the dying teach us about recovering our wholeness? The moment of death stands as a moment of unpretentiousness. It forces us to look directly at what we are. We can carry nothing extra into that moment. It strips us to our bare essentials.

DYING AS A HUMAN BEING

The only way that we can harmonize ourselves with dying is to be completely human in the face of death. All of our end-of-life hopes and expectations come down to this. We can die naturally only as a human being. We will not move easily into death when we attempt to maintain our pretensions and self-images. Dying forces us back to ourselves. This wisdom in dying can equally be applied to how we live. The messages for a sane life and a healthy death are the same.

There is a Zen Buddhist story of a *roshi* who was dying of stomach cancer. (A roshi is an accomplished teacher in the Zen tradition.) A student came to the roshi and asked him if he had prepared himself to die. The roshi said no preparation was needed. The student then asked how the roshi would die. The roshi grabbed his belly and started rolling around on the floor, moaning in agony. He then returned to his chair and looked at the student to see if the student had understood.

The Zen roshi was pointing to the lack of preparation needed for being a human being. Just as there is no right way to die, there is no perfect personality that we have to emulate. All we can do is be who we are, with all of our imperfections and warts, and allow death to take us as it will. For some of us that will mean feeling our fear, depression, and grief. Others will cry out in anger and rage. How we manifest our death is not important because the process will lead us however it unfolds. What is important is letting go of our ideas about how we should be and surrendering to the fullness of our humanity.

Many people have fixed ideas about dying which come from their theological beliefs. When some of these people are forced to confront their emotions surrounding death, they meet death and dying with their ideas rather than their humanness. In hospice work we call this dysfunctional theology. The person's belief structure interferes with his or her humanity. The person defaults to his ideas about how to die rather than allowing himself to feel the intensity of his loss. He begins to dismiss his feelings as being wrong or inappropriate. This leads to an enormous internal struggle because dying will not allow him to dismiss his emotional reactions. It keeps forcing the feelings back into his consciousness.

One hospice patient I worked with was a Christian fundamentalist. Edward believed in the literal word of the Bible and would quote scripture whenever I arrived for a visit. He told me on several occasions that he was going to heaven, and God expected him to be happy because of that prospect. Even his fear was seen in the context of his faith. At night Edward would have nightmares about his death, and in the morning he would quote a line in the Bible about being tempted by the devil in the face of everlasting life. As Edward deteriorated I could feel his growing anguish despite his pretensions to the contrary.

During one of my visits I asked Edward if the love he felt for his family was a gift from God. He nodded. Then I asked if God would want him to acknowledge his love before he left for heaven. He agreed and asked his wife and daughter to come over and be with him. Edward began to tell his family how much he loved them and how desperately he would miss them. He began to open to his grief and broke down sobbing. By allowing his human pain to become part of his dying, Edward came to a greater acceptance of the process of death.

We connect with God through our humanity, not through our beliefs. Being human and fearful of dying does not deny the promise of heaven; in fact, it is only when we recover our naturalness that we can relax into death and find heaven. When we project our ideals onto our concept of heaven, we create an infinite separation between heaven and earth; but when we align with the truth of our human condition, we free ourselves from our painful ideals and rest in the contentment of our hearts. Through our hearts we learn and grow more deeply into our humanity, becoming free to move through the fear that keeps our relationship to death fixed and impersonal.

A few of the most difficult deaths I have witnessed have been of people who defined their death as a spiritual experience. In subtle ways their spiritual definition separated them from the actual experience. They thought they should be calmer, quieter, and more peaceful and equanimous than they were. Inside, their minds were screaming as they pretended to be placid in the face of their demise. How does this false tranquility serve anyone in the face of death? Death is not fooled. It will force us into our screams.

We will suffer in our dying if we refuse to challenge our self-deceptions. If we open in honesty to what is occurring within us, we can end our exile and be born again into our naturalness. Our self-dishonesty cannot survive death. All of our vanity and arrogance fade into humility when we confront death. Death does not allow us the luxury of carrying extra baggage.

We cannot carry our known selves into the source of all unknowing. The known cannot grasp the unknown. The only way to truly meet death is to become the unknown itself. This demands innocence: we must be free of all expectations of death, both good and bad. Otherwise death remains a parallel universe that is always feared and never understood. If we are to have a psychologically easy death, we have to go out of this world as we came in, with a naked and natural mind.

To be completely human when we die does not mean we die without difficulty. It does not mean our minds are blank and our faces serene. Our humanity asks us to let go of our ideals, to let go of the thoughts that keep us distant from our naturalness. When we meet death without expectation there is no difference between how we die and how we would like to die. We no longer struggle against the process because we have attuned ourselves to the way things are.

ADDRESSING OUR FEARS

Our aversion to death is conditioned by all the little ways we avoid disagreeable situations throughout life. It is as if a lifetime of escaping from the unpleasant is squeezed to the surface when we face our mortality. The principal reason we escape from situations is because we are afraid to meet the unknown. We are uncertain how the situation will turn out, so we flee in a known and safe direction, but when we are dying we cannot change our course to make the process safer. This time there is no turning away from the unknown. Death causes an enormous confrontation with our fear of the unknown. As we go through the dying process we project memories of other fearful situations in our life onto our death. Death becomes the target for a lifetime of accumulated fears.

Ruth was a hospice patient and a Holocaust survivor who had been tortured with needles by her German captors during World War II. She was a sweet person who was straightforward and honest in her speech. Ruth had liver cancer, and as it progressed her abdominal area would fill with fluid. This ascites caused her increasing discomfort, and eventually she asked that it be removed. The way a doctor removes the fluid is by using a long syringe and extracting it from the patient's belly. Ruth became very fidgety as the doctor prepared the needle and fell into vivid flashbacks of her imprisonment and torture. This turned to extreme terror as the needle entered her abdominal area. The hospice nurse knelt beside Ruth throughout the ordeal and repeatedly called her by name, saying gently, "You are right here, Ruth. You are not in the concentration camp. Be right here with me. Don't go away to that place. Come back and be right here with me."

When we are dying we are not as well defended psychologically as we normally are. Perhaps the energy that usually maintains our defense mechanisms is being used in working with our death. As in Ruth's example, past memories are not as separated and distinct from the present moment as they usually are. Past and present seem to flow together in a seamless reference to time and in a single stream of consciousness. Moments of our history that are charged with regret and shame are suddenly available and seem to blend into our current thinking. As these previously unconscious memories begin to surface, everything is open to view. Many of our fears flow effortlessly from the shadow into waking consciousness. We are left having to work with a lifetime of unattended issues without our usual defenses.

One hospice patient I worked with for a number of months was Anthony, an elderly man who had been diagnosed with terminal prostate cancer fifteen years earlier. Because of the widespread metastases the doctor, at the time of diagnosis, had given him only weeks to live. After the visit to the doctor, Anthony decided to visit a famous faith healer who was in his area. He was sitting in the balcony of the church when the faith healer looked up in his direction and said, "There is someone here tonight sitting in the balcony who has prostate cancer. Stand up and you will be healed." Anthony said as he stood up his body was filled with light. The next day he returned to the doctor, and the doctor could not find any trace of the cancer. Anthony was so overcome with conviction that he began to bear witness for other faith healers. He did this for fourteen years. Finally he began to feel progressively weaker, and he returned to his physician for consultation. The doctor discovered prostate cancer. Anthony had placed so much of his identity in not having prostate cancer; he refused to believe the diagnosis and told everyone that he had a heart condition. I could feel the internal battle being waged within him as he groped to sustain his faith in the face of his cancer. A few months later Anthony's obituary read that he had died of heart failure.

Sometimes we become so preoccupied with one of our personal roles or self-images that we refuse to allow that image to change. We feel diminished as a person when we have to give up important areas of our identity. Anthony was never able to accommodate his dying because he refused to accept himself with prostate cancer. He would not allow himself to change. He was more interested in maintaining his role than trusting in his adaptability and his humanity.

While we are dying, pieces of our self-image are continually falling away. Our work and sexual identity, our role as parent, spouse, lover, and friend are all called into question. Death strips us down to the bare essentials of being human, yet we are still complete in our humanity.

All the roles we play in life are elaborate decorations to cover over our humanness. We are used to being a wife, a professional, or a mother. Each new role confines us to the behavior appropriate for that role. When our identification with a role is strong, we have little room to connect with what lies beyond. As time goes by and our roles increase in number, our operating space narrows and our freedom diminishes. Our pasture shrinks as we pull in the fences that enclose us. We become cornered by our self-definitions.

To be fully human is to understand the influence of fear. Fear collects in those areas of our life where we are ignorant and have little clarity. Sometimes it indicates where we need to heal. If we fear loneliness or commitment, for example, our fear guides us to develop in these areas. Suppose we have had a history of poor intimacy in relationships. When we start to get involved and begin to feel the old fear of commitment pulling us away, instead of following our old pattern and fleeing from that intimacy, we can use the fear as a signal. The fear cues us to stay alert because we are approaching an edge for our growth. When used in this way fear becomes a tool for growth rather than a limitation.

As the following story illustrates, the same fears that condition us in life can follow us into death. There is no assurance that we will suddenly understand our fears or stop fearing altogether just because our heart stops beating. It is much more likely that after death we will face the same fears as we did before. We sometimes think of death as a respite from the burdens of life, but it may be a change only in the outer garment while the inner process continues. It may be that death challenges our self-images from the new perspective of having a consciousness but no body.

A hospice home health aide was attending a difficult dying person. Edna was a diagnosed schizophrenic and would lie in bed in a fetal position making grunting angry sounds when anyone approached. The rest of the hospice staff grew tired of her kicking and pushing them away. Needless to say, Edna was not a very popular patient, and visits with her were usually shorter and less frequent than with other patients. The hospice aide, however, deliberately stayed with Edna for longer periods of time. After bathing Edna the aide would kneel beside the bed and speak to her in reassuring terms. She would end her time with a kiss on Edna's cheek. Slowly the relationship developed, and Edna no longer struggled when the aide came to her home.

Edna suddenly died late one night. At that same moment in her own house, the aide called out in her sleep, "I am lost. Who am I? Where am I? I can't find my way back!" The spouse of the aide was naturally alarmed and turned on the lights. With the lights on, the aide woke up and said she knew Edna had died. Edna's consciousness seemed to have merged with the consciousness of the aide, and the aide knew that even in death, Edna was lost in her fear.

Whether this particular story speaks clearly to our predicament or not is unimportant. What matters is that we work on our fears now, while we are alive, and let death take care of itself. It appears from many hospice experiences that there is a seamless continuity between life and death. If we take advantage of the challenges that life continually offers, we may establish an attitude for further growth after death. The one common factor that appears to be available both in living and dying is our potential to grow by addressing our fear.

The real mystery in life and death is the riddle of the human mind. Death reveals the way we put ourselves together through a lifetime of fear and attachment. All of our self-concepts, self-images, and identifications are temporary holding patterns preventing us from facing the greater challenge of being a completely natural human being. Once we understand this we can begin to address our self-abuse and seek ways to forgive others and ourselves.

FORGIVENESS

Many adults have a history of childhood abuse. The mistreatment may have been so devastating that they never fully recovered from the trauma. I have seen people work on their "inner child of the past" for many years. Even after years of therapy and meditation the fear and rage can still continue. In the words of one meditation teacher who was abused as a child, "It never goes away completely."

As harmful as these early experiences can be to our psyche, an accompanying form of abuse frequently compounds them. This is the abuse we give ourselves. This form is even more widespread and affects most of us in one way or another. What others have done to us in the past shapes our self-dislike and unworthiness. We add to the enormous sorrow of our childhood, with the lack of compassion for ourselves. Our childhood experiences were time bound; we carry the inner abuser around with us continually. We sometimes hold ourselves accountable for circumstances beyond our control and then abuse ourselves for years over the outcome.

Our hospice grief support group opens its services to the community at large. One evening a man who had not been served by hospice joined the first group session. During the initial meeting each participant shared his or her individual story of grief. This person said that his wife had died five years earlier of Alzheimer's disease. They had been married over fifty years. Before she became ill the couple had pledged to each other that neither one would ever place the other in a nursing home. Soon after that vow his wife started to deteriorate mentally. She could no longer recognize her family, and she would wander away from home and not be able to find her way back. At one point she left the gas burner of the stove on and came close to burning down the house. The couple's grown children and the family physician all encouraged the husband to place his wife in a nursing home. Reluctantly he conceded and placed her in the nicest home he could find. She died two weeks after moving to the home.

At this point in his story the man was crying uncontrollably. He said that he had not lived a single day in the last five years free from the guilt of breaking his vow to his wife. The other people in the group all supported what he had done. One woman suggested the man forgive himself for making the promise in the first place rather than feeling guilty for the action that broke the promise. The man refused to listen to any of their advice and said, "I must live with the guilt of my broken promise for the rest of my life."

We seem to have an unlimited ability to hold ourselves hostage to the past. Since the past is fixed it is unforgiving. It will not give us a second chance to act differently. Our past says that the harm we did is irreparable.

We are prisoners of actions we cannot change. But our perspective of the events can change even though the events themselves cannot.

Guilt arises when we maintain a fixed self-image from past to present. In guilt there is no room for self-improvement or growth, but plenty for self-condemnation. We did something unskillful yesterday or last year, and we blame ourselves today for those past actions. But things are not the same now. We might respond very differently if the same situation occurred today. Why do we linger in guilt about the person we used to be? That person has died, and, by letting go of that image and allowing ourselves to be who we are today, we can experience forgiveness.

The way to understand guilt is not to ignore or repress it but to open it up beyond its content and relationship to time. Since our past actions cannot be changed, to dwell again and again on what we did wrong keeps us imprisoned within immutable time. Struggling in this way only reinforces our bondage. It is another form of self-abuse. Imperfect actions are an indication of our humanness. Very few actions we take are totally pure in attitude and response. To acknowledge that as a human being most of our responses are incomplete and partial is to admit that our growth is unfinished. We have been placed on this earth to grow in an open-ended way, not to be pure.

When we are forgiving, we attempt to forgive those who wrong us for the specific harm they have caused. But incidents of wrongdoing can never be made right. Forgiveness cannot come by addressing a particular incident alone. It can only come by forgiving the character of the person who did the wrong. The character is the sum total of all the person's behavior. We forgive persons for being who they are. We forgive them for not being totally reliable human beings. Such forgiveness is possible only when we have accepted our own character flaws.

In Jean Paul Sartre's play *No Exit*, three dead people find themselves in hell. This hell is not the torturous physical environment often depicted in theologies but the unforgiving attitude of the inhabitants toward one another. These three people cannot tolerate one another but can find no way out of the others' company. The story demonstrates how we each create a hell within the mind. We need no help from an angry and unforgiving deity. The hell we create on earth for one another is a symptom of the private hells we create when we are unable to allow for any transgressions.

We are usually unable to forgive and allow ourselves to be fallible human beings. Because of this harshness, we are not good at forgiving others. We have little room in our hearts for self-acceptance, much less for forgiveness of others. The more we pressure ourselves with our morality, the greater our self-condemnation. When we define ourselves as being on a path of purification, we create a shadow that expects us to be superhuman. The results are shame, guilt, and an unforgiving mind.

Religious morality cannot help us forgive because it imposes an idea of forgiveness that does not come from the heart. "I forgive you because God expects that of me." We attempt to live up to God's standards of tolerance. Such gestures do not come from an open heart but from a prescribed ethical standard. Forgiveness can only arise out of deep humanity. Forgiveness was never divine. It has always arisen from the innocence of heart that gives permission to be fallible.

One of the distressing events in my early adulthood was the death of my mother. I was going to school in Ohio, and my parents were living in Georgia. Occasionally I would fly down to Georgia to visit them on holidays and weekends. On one trip my mother was very ill and had a temperature of over 102 degrees for two weeks. She had seen the doctor a week earlier, and he had diagnosed her illness as influenza. After the second week of this high fever my mother thought that the illness might be more serious than originally diagnosed, and she asked me to call the doctor and report that the fever was continuing. My relationship with my mother at that point in time was strained, and I told her that the doctor had already diagnosed her with the flu, and I did not want to bother him again. She asked me to call him once more, and I reluctantly agreed. When I called him, I phrased the problem as my mother's heightened concern, and said that if he would simply tell her again she had the flu, she would accept it and relax. The doctor told me to tell her it was the flu. I relayed this back to my mother, and she did become more relaxed about her fever. My trip came to an end and I returned home. Two days after I got back I received a call from my brother. My mother had died of pneumonia.

How was I to live with that death? That action would burn in me for years, and I condemned myself cruelly while trying to atone for it in many ways. After years of trying to right the wrong, I saw this could never be done. Self-forgiveness would never come from rationalizing my action or blaming the doctor. It could only come from the wisdom of time, from watching my actions, knowing my intentions, and seeing the incomplete results. Having high ideals just seemed to cause more inward conflict. Since I could never live up to my expectations of myself, there was nothing left to do but allow myself to make mistakes and learn from them all along the way.

I found I became more accepting of my mistakes when my intention was to learn from them. I saw I usually did the best I could, given the circumstances—my mood, my confused relationships with others, my past history. Out of all of that I would act, and often the action was incomplete. What more could I do but attempt to learn and begin again.

We all do the best we can. When we see this in others, our hearts open. When we see it in ourselves, we can begin to forgive. True, our actions are often incomplete and hurtful. We may be lost in a selfish state of mind, but often that is all the clarity our minds will allow. Because of our limited understanding in that moment, there is no other way we can act. But realizing this is only the beginning of the process of self-knowledge.

Over time we begin to view ourselves with a little more compassion. We start by being tolerant. For many people this is difficult to do, so we develop tolerance for our intolerance. We own our prejudice. Saying "I should not be like this" simply conditions more intolerance in our minds. Instead we might open to our mind's darkest corners, allowing the shadow to come into the light of our attention. Awareness of our states of mind is the light that heals. Awareness is its own protection from acting irresponsibly.

To excuse our behavior by saying "Oh, that's just the way I am" is to dismiss our responsibility for being the way we are. It is a deflection away from who we are by providing an excuse and a rationale for what we do. When we fully accept who we are we do not need an excuse; everything we do is totally acknowledged and owned. We live with ourselves just the way we are, intensely studying our reactions and responses. We honor ourselves as growing human beings and take responsibility for acting according to that humanity.

Being natural also includes holding ourselves and others accountable for inappropriate behavior. Many of the behaviors that we have endured cannot be easily forgiven. We take responsibility for our lack of forgiveness and hold others accountable for their actions. This could take the form of either confronting or avoiding the person altogether. But our actions are based on being a responsible human being and not on a prescribed reaction. Forgiveness is possible only when we take full responsibility without deflecting the blame or rationalizing our behavior.

Being natural is open-ended forgiveness. It is living a life as a human being without internal contradiction. It is both being simple and simply being who we are without pretension or exaggeration. We own our mistakes without condemnation because we are interested in self-growth, not self-abuse. Forgiveness flows easily from ourselves to other people because our hearts are not involved in any internal conflict.

Bearing Our Humanity

Reflect on what it means to be natural. Some people think of being natural in stereotypical terms, such as being a hippie or living off the land. But is that what we really mean by living naturally? Are you aware that there are times when you are unable to be casual and unconstrained? Why does it seem so difficult to be who you are? Consider the meaning of the word spontaneity, and look at your life to see where and when you are spontaneous. Do the expectations of others seem to affect your ability to be natural? Reflect on the times you are most comfortable with other people. What allowed you to feel comfortable?

Pick a role that you assume every day, such as boss, parent, spouse, lover, or friend. Watch the expectations that others have of you in fulfilling that role. Feel the internal pressure you place on yourself. Experience the value and limitations of those expectations. Can you assume the responsibility of that role without the expectations or self-imposed pressure? How does this change the nature of your internal responses to the role? Does it affect the functions you fulfill in the role itself?

Reflect on how and when you pretend to be other than who you are, such as when you were vulnerable or ill. Did you attempt to be stronger and more self-reliant than you felt, or did you project more dependency and helplessness than was needed? What are the payoffs and rewards for pretending that you are needier or stronger than you feel?

The next time you are in a vulnerable position watch carefully for any overplaying of the situation. Remember that naturalness implies self-honesty, so be very honest throughout this exercise. Do you intentionally try to draw other people into your drama by exaggerating your predicament or, conversely, do you shun all outside help? Do you try to appear stronger or weaker than you feel? Are you able to be aware of this pattern? Are you willing to let go of this tendency?

Reflect upon your idea of a perfect death. Would it be sudden or prolonged? If you had time to adjust, how would you act as a dying patient on your last day of life? Would you be serene and composed, affectionately welcoming everyone to your bedside? How would you leave this earth? Who would be by your side, and what would you be saying to them? Is this ideal possible or even approachable?

The next time you are sick, compare how you behave with your ideal scenario. Take a few minutes and use your illness to practice dying. For this short period of time, let go of the desire to get better. Surrender to the weakness of the body. Watch the sluggishness of the mind. Does this make you feel out of control? What emotions arise during this exercise? Recognize that whatever emotional and physical problems occur probably pale by comparison to the difficulties you will face in dying.

Reflect on self-forgiveness. How much forgiveness do you have for your past transgressions? Think of something you did in the past that has weighed on your consciousness. Do not excuse or rationalize what you did. Take full responsibility. Is it possible to forgive and take full responsibility? What happens to self-forgiveness when you blame or excuse the action away? Reflect on the difference between the person you are now and the person you were then.

Go through an old family photo album. Look at the scenes and events pictured and try to remember the emotions and the difficulties of family life during that period. Remember what you were like back then, and recall some of the things you did that were less than kind. Remember the stresses you were under and the problems you were facing. Now bring that growing child into your heart. Allow that struggling child to be fallible. You were doing the best you could to survive. Understand the reasons why you acted as you did, and forgive this person who you no longer are.

6 | Learning from Every Experience

People travel to wonder at the height of mountains,
at the huge waves of the sea, at the long courses
of rivers, at the vast compass of ocean, at the circular
motions of the stars: and they pass by themselves
without wondering.

—SAINT AUGUSTINE

YEAR AFTER YEAR throughout our lives we accumulate a body of knowledge that we believe will help us to succeed in one endeavor or another. Academic achievement is rewarded, and advanced degrees are essential for many of the most desired professional positions in society. We have grown accustomed to relying heavily on our knowledge, and in many ways we treat knowledge like a commodity; it becomes one of our many acquisitions. As we learn from the dying, however, the most valuable learning is not about memorizing facts and figures. It is not about higher grade-point averages and accumulating degrees. It is about life itself, and its impact is on the heart.

Liam, a hospice patient and friend, was moved by a letter he received while he was dying. The letter said that life is filled with little deaths before the big death. Liam reflected on this and inquired deeply into the message. He began to understand that life was about releasing the world to die in each moment. The hospice nurse attending Liam said that he was very passionate about learning as much about life in his final days as he possibly could. She was amazed at the intensity of his inquiry. During the last few days of life he seemed to realize fully the meaning of the quotation. Liam died peacefully and quietly in his home.

Life is a process and not a product. We encounter it as a continual series of beginnings and endings. When we experience these changes, we open to all the little deaths before the big death. These deaths force us to conclude that life is not about possessing objects or obtaining a good reputation. All of our achievements, wealth, worries, plans, expectations, regrets, status, and prestige are over when we die. Death and change inevitably strip them from our life. Since all things are finite, acquiring them cannot give us lasting satisfaction. Death will take them away and reveal our misplaced focus. When we begin to understand this lesson of death, we change our orientation to all experiences.

The dying frequently reorient themselves in this way. They ponder their accomplishments in light of their inevitable death and begin to question deeply the meaning of their lives. Like my friend Liam, they sometimes turn inward and attempt to come to terms with the lost years that were focused on transitory gain and status. Surprisingly, instead of lingering amid regrets, patients often emerge from this period of reflection with a greater joy and fuller sense of participation than they have ever had.

John, one of our hospice patients, experienced this change. He was a successful banker, raised a nice family, and was held in high esteem by his neighbors and friends. He was in the later stages of lung cancer when our hospice started serving him. When John's illness progressed to the point where he could no longer maintain the denial of his death, he fell into a deep despair. He talked about his depression with his social worker. John said he had worked hard to achieve his success. He wondered what it had all been about. How were all his possessions going to help him now? His dying was difficult because it showed him his whole life in perspective and led him to reevaluate all his assumptions. The next week the social worker returned and found John in a very upbeat mood. John said he "gave up" his depression when he realized he had spent his whole life regretting his past. His depression was just more of the same. John had decided to discover a new way to live.

It took a terminal illness for John to question his life assumptions. The "American Dream," which he had pursued with such enthusiasm, turned into a nightmare when he confronted his death. He was able to change his life dramatically from product to process once he saw the limitations of his old lifestyle. He seemed to realize that lamenting his past was as useless as mourning a loss in the stock market—something he had considerable experience in doing.

There is immense subtlety in how we use life as a commodity. Our tendency to treat life itself as a possession follows us into virtually every action we take. Even the expressions we use, such as "wasting" or "saving time," act as the foundation on which we build further products. Our attempt to hold and maintain life as a possession is not limited to the material world around us. We also attempt to hold on to pleasant emotions and avoid unpleasant feelings as well. We seek happiness and shun pain. We want peace and dislike confusion. We tell ourselves that if we just maintain the right attitude, our happiness will continue and we will avoid unpleasant moods entirely.

But the products of the world inevitably decay. Try as we will, we cannot save a single thing from death. Death stalks us in the middle of our happiness, it is there when we finally gain the recognition we deserve, and it is continually working during the depression and elation that we think will last forever. Ultimately we cannot be satisfied with pursuing life as a thing, for the pleasures we seek so desperately will ultimately die, if we do not go first.

This process eventually leads us to experience the world of things and ideas as fundamentally flawed. What good is life when everything dies? With this discovery, some people become cynical about all forms of happiness; others attribute the flaws they see to their own imperfection and resolve to try harder. But life is not flawed; what is defective is the strategy we employ to engage it. Acquiring things will never lead to complete contentment. This is one of the great lessons we learn from the dying and from the impermanent nature of all existence.

The question then arises, what will lead to happiness? What orientation to life will free us from the influence of death? What direction could we possibly take that will not be just another form of the same acquiring mentality? Is it possible to develop an attitude that focuses on being alive rather than on accumulating and possessing life?

USING LIFE FOR LEARNING

The dying teach us that we cannot find contentment in our possessions. They point to something that lies beyond our need to acquire, to something much less tangible but ultimately more fulfilling. The dying direct us toward relationships as the reason for being alive. Relationship is not just people caring about people, although that certainly is important, but the ability to relate to everything, to be open, to learn and grow through every situation and circumstance.

Like Liam and John, whose passion for learning culminated in their peaceful death, the dying often seem to be searching for the clues of a process that will take them beyond this world. They search for this everywhere, in conversations, books, and deeply within themselves. Some find it, some do not. Those who do seem to see through the outer skin of life and look into the substance beyond appearances. They are no longer interested in being bound to their environment but in setting themselves free to move as circumstances demand.

Eleanor was a hospice patient who had been a history teacher for thirty years before cancer forced her retirement. She entertained the visiting hospice staff with stories from her life, always connecting them with themes from world history. In the beginning the history stories were usually anecdotal and either humorous or morally instructive. As Eleanor's illness progressed, the staff became aware of a different tone to her tales. There was more urgency, and the lessons became more philosophical and poignant. She started to draw her analogies from Plato, Socrates, or Christian saints. She believed history could lead her through her dying and demonstrate a perspective that would help her. She was working on herself even as she was telling her stories, groping for themes that would allow her to rest and relax into her dying.

One day as the hospice nurse was visiting, Eleanor began speaking metaphorically about her dying when she suddenly stopped. Her eyes were bright and flashing. She looked at the nurse and said, "I suddenly understand what it has all been about! It has been about the very learning itself. I kept wanting to find a lesson that would give me comfort, but the learning is the lesson. . . . Never forget," she added, as if to remind herself, "Life is about learning."

The nurse said Eleanor was like a little child in the excitement of her discovery. Eleanor felt her revelation penetrated the depth of what life was about. From that time on she never told another story to the staff. It was as if the stories had led her to this conclusion and were no longer needed.

We have all had this childlike excitement at one time or another. When we are young we have a passion for understanding and growth. Infants and toddlers continually engage the world through handling, manipulating, and peering at objects in front of them. Learning is as natural as breathing and is inherent in the developmental process. Children's minds are instinctively curious and inquisitive, and self-education comes naturally.

Childhood is a time of great wonder as the mysteries of the world begin to reveal themselves and unfold into further questions. We grow with a refreshing desire to understand the world around us. Our discoveries lead to a great deal of joy and enthusiasm for life. Children never seem to tire of discovering new objects. Learning appears to add vitality to their minds. Perhaps what we think of as childhood exuberance and energy is due more to having a mind that is open and learning than to youthful vigor.

As we become socialized, learning for its own sake begins to be replaced by learning in order to acquire knowledge. Learning becomes tied to a goal; our need for social acceptance and self-worth supersedes our inherent wonder. Competition inside the classroom gradually replaces our natural urgency to understand the world.

As we tie additional incentives to what we learn and reward knowledge, we begin to lose the joy of curiosity. Information rather than learning becomes the primary objective of study. Learning becomes secondary to a conditioned pleasure in possessing information as we rely increasingly on knowledge for our safety and security. The natural process of learning with all of its vitality is lost to us, and we become increasingly dull.

Most of us use our acquired knowledge to make decisions and determine how we will act throughout the day. We search our personal histories for similar problems and act from that past blueprint. Children have very brief histories so their responses are more spontaneous and natural. They learn as they go, relying less on their knowledge and more on what seems appropriate in the immediate situation. But adults rely heavily on experience to carry them through the day. Knowledge and information are essential for all of us to master the world of objects, work on our jobs, recognize people, and find our way back home. Reading, studying, and accumulating information is essential to our survival as a species. Knowledge, however, is not alive. It is the product of past learning and therefore dead. Because it applies what we did in the past to what is happening now, it can inhibit our current range of responses. We end up seeing the unknown present in terms of the known past and lose our edge of mystery and wonder.

If we want to keep a sense of wonder alive and active, we will use our knowledge to inform decisions but not determine them. Life is in constant movement. To remain vitally alive, we must act spontaneously relative to that movement. We inhibit our responses when we base our actions solely on knowledge. When we spend time weighing alternatives, the opportunities within the moment quickly escape us. We feel distant and remote from the vital flow of life, which is instantaneous and immediate. Our hearts remain hidden by the abstract world of our thinking mind with their opinions, ideas, and assumptions.

I have seen many people die who have spent their lives cultivating their intellects at the expense of their hearts. They are unable to meet their death with the open-hearted response that it requires. Their deaths are fearful and irresolute because ideas by themselves cannot do anything. We use ideas to do things. People who live only in their intellect cannot handle the emotional impact of losing all the knowledge they have spent their lifetime cultivating. By covering their hearts they have suffocated their learning attitude—the only expression of life that can lead to a fulfilling death.

As a hospice social worker, I worked with Thomas, a forty-three-year-old lawyer with a wonderful wife and two small children. Thomas fought his cancer with all his physical and mental strength. He permitted hospice to serve him only after the urging of his wife and doctor. Thomas was so preoccupied with the latest knowledge of any new alternative therapy that he had little time left for his family. They desperately wanted and needed his attention. His five-year-old son would take the medical text that Thomas spent most of his time mulling over and hide it under the chair. Once, after hiding the book, the child crawled onto the bed with his father hoping he would respond. Thomas was too absorbed to even notice his son. When Thomas became too tired to read for himself, he would have his wife read the newest medical journals to him. Thomas died restless and agitated, fighting his death to the end, and his family was never able to bring closure to his illness.

Thomas missed the opportunity to share his last days fully with his family. His consuming appetite for knowledge frustrated his wife and children and closed him off from the natural learning available to him, the lessons of the heart. The very quality of life he sought from his texts was available from the love his family was offering.

Genuine learning is always a process and never a commodity. Far from being an intellectual pursuit, it is the art of being alive. It is the active participation in living relationships. Learning connects us with the ongoing movement of life without trying to freeze our relationship to that movement. There are no mistakes in learning because every success or failure is more food for learning. If we do poorly on an exam, lose our self-respect, receive criticism from our boss, or err in our marriage, it is all nourishment for our growth. Learning is open-ended and is never completed. If we attempt to cash in our chips and pull away from learning, we are left with our pot of knowledge, but we will have disconnected ourselves from our hearts.

Learning is not cumulative; it does not lead to something else. We cannot amass it as we can knowledge. It is immediate and momentary. It impacts not only our minds but the core of our being. All learning, no matter how mundane the topic, is spiritual because it transforms us into something more than we were.

Fear often accompanies growth because there are no guarantees on how we will grow. There is no safety in learning. We may grow away from our patterns, prejudices, and belief systems; we do not know. If we steer our growth in a predetermined direction—grow according to a plan we have in mind, keeping our hands always on the controls—we eliminate the mystery and end up calculating our future even as we think we are being open and exploring. When we learn we welcome the return of the mystery. It is the only approach that meets life with the trust it deserves.

The hospice chaplain had been seeing Alice, a patient who was hospitalized for her end-stage cancer. The hospital staff was reluctant to enter Alice's room because of her anger and hostility. Alice acted prejudiced and accusatory toward everyone. During one of the chaplain's visits, Alice started talking about a verse in the Bible that spoke about Jesus healing people by casting out the demons. Alice asked the chaplain, "Do you think I have demons?" The chaplain, assessing that the patient was ready to hear, responded, "Yes, I do." Alice quickly asked what kind of demons she had. The chaplain said, "You have the demons of anger, bigotry, and lack of forgiveness." To the surprise of the chaplain, Alice responded, "Please, let us pray together. I do not want to die with those demons." The chaplain later recalled how Alice had seemed to heal many of her old wounds in the weeks before her death.

Alice was forced to confront herself through her dying. This reluctant confrontation infused her with a new motivation: to learn and to set herself on a course away from her demons. She was not certain how she would grow. She only knew that her lifelong emotional suffering was intolerable. In the face of her death Alice was willing to move beyond her self-imposed limitations and allow her intuitive heart to guide her.

THE KNOWN AND THE UNKNOWN

In our culture there is tremendous power and status in being someone who knows. We often hear that knowledge is power and relate to our universities the way medieval culture did to cathedrals. We honor people for what they already know rather than for their spontaneous wisdom. We feel as if we are giving up a position of strength when we are not acting from our store of knowledge. We are afraid of being seen as weak or, worse, insignificant. Our self-identity is built around what we know, and we feel empowered when information is within easy access.

A strongly opinionated person often feels extreme isolation and disconnection. The more we know about something the less open we are to approaching it with an innocent mind, and the further it seems to recede from our hearts. We try to overcome this separation by gaining more knowledge about the object, but this only widens the distance between the object and ourselves. Our attempts to decrease this isolation by acquiring knowledge continue until we tire from the pain of our loneliness.

When we are learning, we feel the full impact of life because we are open and allow the world into our consciousness completely. There is no distance from the object at all; we absorb the total experience like a sponge, without evaluating or comparing it to a previous one. A learning moment is a moment of innocence. When Christ said, "Lest we be like little children, we cannot enter the kingdom of God," perhaps he was speaking of this orientation to learning.

I was a social worker for Linda, a dying thirty-three-year-old wife and mother of two young children. As Linda approached her death, she requested our inpatient services rather than remaining at home to die. When Linda entered our facility she started to actively die. Several hospice staff gathered in her room, everyone holding hands encircling the bed. Most patients who are dying are unable to describe their process because they are in a coma or too weak to communicate. Linda was neither. She began to describe the experience of dying. This is a hospice staff's dream come true. Most hospice workers have chosen this occupation because of their fascination and curiosity with the process of dying. Finally here was someone able to describe death in detail as it was occurring. "I cannot feel the sense of touch anymore," Linda said. "I cannot see.... There is no hearing now.... My God, I am no longer in my body." Then she tried to say something more but died in that instant.

I looked around the room at my colleagues standing by the bed. We were all in rapt attention, keenly focused, absorbed, and totally receptive. One staff member said later, "Each word Linda spoke was touching my heart like a drumbeat. It was as if the secrets of the universe were being revealed." All of us were on the edge of what we knew about life and death, and Linda was whispering the clues that we had long been seeking. It was a moment that deeply affected us all.

As I left that death, I reflected on the number of opportunities we have each and every moment to open to the secrets of the universe. It occurred to me that knowledge always leads to greater wonder as long as we use it as a platform on which to continue to learn. If we allow knowledge to guide our questioning, it returns us to the innocence of learning. Only our arrogance, our belief that we know more than the moment can teach us, holds us back from the childlike learning of long ago. At some point we have allowed ourselves to lose this childhood orientation to self-growth and substituted adult ego fulfillment. Sadly we call this maturity.

Frequently we are more interested in teaching than in learning, in speaking than in listening. We want to teach and speak as a way of staking out our position. Our stance in life can be so active and assertive that we forget the value of being open and receptive. It is possible to learn as we teach and speak, but to do so requires that we are self-aware and open to feedback. It is never our actions that disrupt the learning but our inability to listen in innocence from within those actions. When we release ourselves into this innocence we free everything in the world to resume its place in the mystery of things.

The unknown is the source of all learning. Learning is a death in itself because we directly contact the unknown. It is a mini-death, a death within life. Every death is a birth into something new, and every birth is a death of the familiar. We go naked into our learning as we do when we die. When we carry our residual knowledge into learning, we are trying to shield ourselves from the death of that moment. We inevitably try to make every mini-death a safe passage by bringing along part of ourselves. We can ward off death, we feel, by bringing our knowledge along with us. Knowledge becomes a form of security protecting us from the unknown.

Through our beliefs in an afterlife, we attempt to make death known. But the beauty (and horror) of death is that it remains unknowable. Death cannot be known because everything we know ends with death.

The question is not whether there is an afterlife but what is our relationship with the unknown. There are many books that attempt to explore the after-death experience. We can rest on these beliefs in an attempt to make death a known and safe subject, but in doing so we misplace the real teaching of death. We may have had psychic or near-death experiences that attest to a continuation of consciousness after we die, but that is not the point. The question is, can we live without projecting anything at all onto the unknown?

When the Buddha was asked about theoretical issues such as whether there was an afterlife, he would not answer. Perhaps he did not want to establish another experience for people to pursue as a diversion from his teaching. He seemed to be saying that if we practice his teaching of the unknown now, what is beyond physical death will take care of itself.

One hospice patient named Timothy was obsessed with maintaining his life as it was. He disliked anyone disturbing any part of his physical environment, and he would get upset if any procedure was altered or his schedule was delayed. He confided in the nurse that he believed in an afterlife and was not afraid of death itself. But he was afraid that after his death he would not be the same person he was now. Timothy confessed that he feared the disorientation and confusion of not having the same points of reference. Even the thought of heaven was partially unpleasant to him because it was an unfamiliar place.

Timothy was fearful of losing everything he understood and wanted to go through death undisturbed. Stories of an afterlife did not calm his fears because in heaven he would be forced to learn a whole new set of operating procedures. Timothy wanted to take this life, just as it was, into the next. As he came ever closer to death and felt his physical strength and mental acuity wane, his fears increased. We all felt helpless as Timothy suffered a great deal in his last weeks of life.

LEARNING FROM DEATH

A spiritual teacher once remarked that our time here on earth is a time to learn about ourselves. But instead of using it as a schoolroom, he said, we use it as a field for competition. If we do well we are happy. If not, we consider ourselves a failure. We hold our self-esteem captive to the outcome of our struggle rather than learning about why we struggle in the first place. Instead of rising and falling with each success and failure, we can learn about how the life strategies we employ limit our freedom and enjoyment. When learning becomes our focus, all mistakes are seen as further opportunities to learn rather than as conclusions about who we are.

Death and dying are opportunities to see these strategies in an intimate way. Death is such an enormous threat to the ego that it acts like an echo chamber for all our concerns, mirroring our intentions, confusions, and fears. Death and dying offer an opportunity to see ourselves up close, with our defenses exposed.

We frequently employ magical ways of thinking to avoid confronting our fears. If we ignore death, we think, we will somehow postpone having to die. At some point it dawns on us that pushing death out of our consciousness forces it to appear in other areas of our lives. Perhaps we develop a heightened concern for our safety and comfort or for our youth and vigor. When we repress our fear of death, fear of survival begins to haunt us.

We cannot force our readiness to learn about death. We become ready when we have seen the limits of our old forms of avoidance. When the adaptive strategies that we have employed to keep death safe and distant no longer work for us, we see that they never really served the function for which they were intended: protecting us from the unknown and pushing death out of reach.

Death and dying is a subject that we may approach with much interest and excitement, for we feel that a great mystery is about to unfold. Many hospice volunteers find joy in touching this subject for the first time. Their joy comes from the heart moving into a previously forbidden subject. As one hospice volunteer put it, "There is a sense of being more alive and participating in a discovery."

This sense of excitement can change into despair and grief as the glow of working with the dying fades into the truth of what this mystery contains. We wanted to learn, but not about this! Many hospice staff find themselves facing an accumulation of grief after about six months of hospice work. This is a crucial time when the initial romanticism of working with the dying must give way to the difficult task of opening our lives to death.

It was mid-December, the holiday season. I had been in hospice work for about six months—months filled with inward conflict and turmoil. Death and dying were a tragedy to me, and I questioned how anyone could possible be happy during this Christmas season in the face of so much suffering and pain. I was walking across the campus of Rice University, reflecting on my grief, when I spotted a father rolling a ball back and forth to his very young son. The son and the father were laughing and enjoying themselves enormously. Despite my disdain for anything that might shake my melancholy, I suddenly realized I was missing something. I had closed down to the joy that balances the grief of dying. I had been caught in a dark drama of my own making. Consumed by the fear and injustice of death, I had been seeing life and death as inimical opposites.

An enormous amount of growth occurs when we learn from death without making something tragic out of it. Healing the rift between life and death means discovering how each complements the other in a complete union. While this is not an easy task, it is not an impossible one either. And once this healing occurs, everything changes with it. The ego, which initially seizes death as a drama, now uses it as a tool for understanding its own nature. Thereafter, death begins to influence our lives in more subtle ways. It is no longer seen as an enemy but as a friend that will guide us toward greater wisdom.

With this new understanding we begin to question every assumption about life. Everything is reexamined and opened to inquiry. Nothing can be taken for granted or assumed to be true because others say it is so. We feel alone, naked, and somewhat vulnerable. Other people do not seem to understand. The only thing we can rely on with assurance is our learning attitude. A massive cultural denial of death influences the way we understand the existence of all things. This great cover-up has now been revealed.

Learning from the Unknown

Reflect on how you use life as a commodity. The product mentality can be subtle. It includes gaining an advantage, attempting to save time, acquiring knowledge, impressing someone, beautifying ourselves. Think about the motivation and intention behind your activities. Are most of your actions focused on gaining or avoiding something? Most forms of deceit come from trying to gain an advantage. Reflect on how much of your life is used in this way. What happens to other people who get in the way? Are the means you employ worth the pain they cause?

Sit quietly alone in an environment free from distractions. Open your senses to the present moment. Hear the sounds, see the objects, smell the odors, feel what is happening within you as you sit quietly. Based on your immediate sense experience, ask yourself what there is to gain or acquire in this moment. What can be added or eliminated to improve what is already occurring? Does your wish to change this moment detract from your ability to experience it?

Reflect on the differences between learning and knowledge. Do you allow yourself to be affected and altered by learning, or do you only store what you learn in your mind to be used as information? What is the motivation behind your curiosity? Think of a time when you were positively changed by an experience. What happened in that moment? Was it knowledge or learning that changed you?

The next time you receive criticism about your actions or your character, try not to dismiss what you hear or defend yourself in any way. It is difficult to be open to another person's criticism without immediately judging that person and rejecting the information. Do not assume the information is true or false, but investigate for yourself. Ask others for their feedback as well. If there is a consistent message and a change is needed, how will you go about changing?

Reflect on your relationship with the unknown. Recall times in your childhood when you faced an unknown moment. How did you act? Was that moment comfortable? As an adult are you more or less open to the unknown than you were as a child? Think about occasions in your present life for experiencing the unfamiliar. Do you approach such opportunities, or avoid them? What holds you back? In the past, have you lost opportunities to learn because of your inaction and fear?

Set aside twenty minutes to be alone without any distractions. Imagine you are dying. See the scene just as it might unfold. What fears are present as your time to die approaches? See yourself going through death to whatever is on the other side. Watch your tendency to fill this unknowable moment with your beliefs. Do you believe in rebirth, resurrection, heaven, nothingness? Why fill the unknown moment of death with anything at all? Imagine the scene again, and this time be aware and die without any projection into the future. You die and that is all. How does this second death compare with the first?

7 | Listening from the Heart

Siddhartha listened. He was now listening intently,
completely absorbed, quite empty, taking in everything.
He felt that he had now completely learned the art
of listening. He had often heard all this before,
all the numerous voices in the river, but today they
sounded different. He could no longer distinguish the
different voices. . . . They all belonged to each other:
the lament of those that yearn, the laughter of the wise,
the cry of indignation and the groan of the dying.
—HERMANN HESSE, *SIDDHARTHA*

WHEN WE ARE COMMITTED to learning for its own sake rather than accumulating knowledge, every experience becomes a teacher. Learning from our interpersonal relationships becomes a priority because much of our lives is spent with other people. In fact we are always in relationship regardless of whether we are with people or alone.

The greatest gift we can offer is the gift of our understanding. Each of us in our hearts seeks to be understood, for to be understood is to be loved. Understanding requires the total participation of the mind and heart of the listener. There can be no evaluation or judgment, just listening with caring attention. The speaker can then grow naturally in whatever way is most appropriate.

Working with the dying shows us how we can learn to listen more effectively. When people die they often reach out for somebody to make the journey with them. Most people prefer companionship to isolation. Dying alone is more feared than dying in physical pain. To be with a person who is dying requires listening beyond our usual means. It means crossing from our territory into his and being with him in his aloneness. Often this requires extra effort, for we must pierce our resistance to being alone.

In the Thai language the word for understanding can be literally translated as "entering the heart." Allowing a person to enter the heart means that our heart is large enough to contain more than our self-interests. When we understand something we allow it to be itself. We place no demands upon it and ask nothing from it in return. Listening requires such an effort. Our heart becomes vulnerable to the pain of another. We feel her suffering, and her pain affects us. We do not try to take it away because we are listening; we are participating, without reacting.

It is very difficult to listen because we keep getting in the way of what we hear. In hospice work, for instance, the dying patient may choose not to take medications. Everyone on a patient's hospice team wants that person to be physically comfortable, but unless we try to understand why the patient chooses to be noncompliant, our efforts will frequently be met with more rigidity from the patient. The patient may want to feel pain because it reminds her that she is still alive. Or the pain might allow her to feel she is atoning for the sins of a lifetime.

In either case, sitting with the person and building a trusting relationship will allow the exploration of these issues. But if the issues are explored with the intent to change the dying person's mind, listening becomes a form of manipulation. We pretend to be neutral on the outcome of the discussion, but in fact we usually want the patient to die our death. We hope to push him subtly toward our definition of salvation. But if we remain vigilant about our own prejudices, we will not contaminate and disturb the listening.

Usually we listen from our own agenda. No matter what the occasion, we judge and evaluate what the person is saying in relationship to our own opinions, to our own standards and measurement. We listen through the screen of our own intentions, waiting for the person to stop speaking so we can assert our own point. Our motivation is often to persuade rather than understand. Frequently we treat the speaker as an adversary rather than a welcome friend. So we may hear little of what is said, and understand even less. In dismissing a person's words, we dismiss the person.

But escaping our biases is not easy. Our opinions influence our listening in subtle ways. No one benefits when we ignore our prejudices or pretend that we have transcended them, for they still color our listening. The only way a prejudice can be neutralized is by owning it as part of our consciousness. It is possible to hear through our opinions, much as we are able to focus our vision on an external object and still be aware of the background.

I was once visiting Lisa, the spouse of a patient who was very close to death. She was an astute and sensitive woman who was very honest and open with her feelings. We had met several times, and each time Lisa grieved intensely. We were sitting facing each other, and I started our conversation by leaning toward her with my arms resting on my legs. I was expecting Lisa to continue her grief work. Lisa looked at me and said, "You know, when you sit like that you force me to grieve. Today I am not feeling sad. I want to talk about other things." In that moment I was clearly not being present with Lisa. All our past sessions together were coloring my availability to her in that instant. I was taken by how subtle my habitual actions may influence and persuade a person in some unconscious way.

PROJECTIONS

Most of us think of reality as an external objective truth. Reality for us is the same as reality for everyone else. It is simply the way we perceive events. Few of us consider that our perceptions could be distorted. We believe that everyone hears or sees in the same way. This limited view of reality is dangerous precisely because we believe it is objective. We do not even realize that we are looking at life through our own prism.

Our perceptions are actually colored by our experiences, opinions, history, and values. For example, when we walk into a dying patient's home, and he is in pain, we bring with us our history of bruised knees and dental appointments. We react out of our personal struggle with pain rather than from the clarity of seeing things the way they are. We end up perceiving only what our mind allows us to see. Instead of letting perceptions come to us, we go out and distort them. We actively influence our reality to fit our preconceived notions and then assume that our embellished version is true. Only when we acknowledge our distortions and prejudices do we begin to free ourselves from their influence.

We are controlled by what we do not include. Most of us have parts of ourselves that we dislike. For some it is our anger or rage; for others it is jealousy and lust. It does not matter what the trait is; it is what we do with it that makes it a problem. Disliking these qualities does not make them go away; it just obscures their influence. When we are averse to these qualities, we attempt to drive them from our consciousness. We deny ownership of them by projecting them onto other people. They are still in us, but by casting them onto someone else, we can react and dislike the other person rather than ourselves.

I worked with Tom, the son of a hospice patient, who I initially thought was a very concerned and loving caregiver. He would appear constantly at the side of his dying mother, catering to her every wish. As I got to know Tom, this constant attention seemed too solicitous. Something did not ring true. It was revealed through our conversations that Tom was a battered child and was harboring enormous hostility toward his mother. He was never able to admit to his anger because it would have been too overwhelming. Tom also became suspicious when other family members spent a lot of time caring for his mother. He felt they would not treat her as well as he did and occasionally accused them of mistreating her. He was, I thought, disowning his anger, displacing it onto other family members, and then overcompensating with excessive caring behavior of his own.

So long as we project our traits onto other people, we remain bound by their power. Battling to escape their control over us, we expend enormous energy to maintain the illusion that these qualities are "out there" rather than originating within us. Touching those disliked areas of ourselves with the same kindness that we show the dying patient is the all-important first step on the road to recovering these rejected parts. Allowing ourselves to see and feel these qualities within our consciousness gives us the freedom to recognize their existence and act differently. Although we may fear being overwhelmed if we allow them access to our consciousness, by not owning them, as we have seen, we imprison ourselves within their energy. Awareness liberates us from their power and makes us whole and total. We can then listen from our heart rather than react from our mind because we have owned all parts of ourselves.

I was teaching a recent workshop for people who were interested in the issues of death and dying. One of the participants, a hospice nurse, expressed guilt and shame for her inability to be present for her patients day after day. I suggested she treat herself as kindly as she treats a dying patient. I asked if she would ever offer the dying the same unforgiving attitude she was inflicting on herself. Later she wrote me the following note: "Thank you deeply for your suggestion to treat myself as a hospice patient. I have intuitively treated hospice patients with a spaciousness and allowance that I do not extend to myself. Are we not all a heartbeat away from dying? Why wait? Why not accord every person and ourselves that same compassion while we are fully engaged in life? Yes!"

LISTENING TO THE DYING

When we sit with the dying we need all our skills to keep from being swept away by the drama in front of us. Dying accentuates almost everyone's problems. Mild emotions grow more volatile and extreme, small incidents become overblown. This is true for the patient, the family and friends, and the caregiver. Death squeezes our unresolved issues to the surface. Because it is the complete and total ending of life, one of the predominant emotions for many people who are dying is fear. Our unreconciled life issues are laced with the intensity of our fear of dying. The compounding of fear and unresolved issues creates a situation of intense unpredictability.

The hospice staff came into this situation not only with their own historical issues around death but with the additional task of trying to provide a calming reassurance to the patient and family throughout their ordeal. A more experienced caregiver has probably been through several hundred deaths, and though these deaths have imparted a familiarity with the process, they have also left their toll on the worker's accumulated grief. Through all of this inward and outward emotional residue the worker's job is to start afresh with each new family.

Listening to the dying involves listening to the person and simultaneously listening to our own reactions. The two are easily confused, since the intensity of the situation causes a heightened form of projection and bias. Our fear of dying, our aversion and denial, color and filter the reality. So many traps lie along the path to clear listening that it is a wonder we ever connect at all beyond our own needs.

Elisabeth Kübler-Ross tells the story of a young mother who was dying. Every person who came into the room entered with the reactions and feelings they had about the death of a young mother: pity, anger, fear, and sadness. The young woman complained that everyone was entering her room to be with their preset feelings. Few came to be with her.

We all know people who have physical or psychological traits that provoke a reaction in us. For some of us it is the disfigured burn patient, for others the person caught in his rage. We usually turn away because we are repulsed by the idea of ourselves being like this person. We react because the issue that confronts us outwardly exposes us to our worst fears. Dying is such a condition. As long as the person is much older we can tolerate being with her. Her age confirms that death is far away from us. But what about the dying patient who is of the same age as us or shares the same life circumstances? Such patients often create the most intense reactions.

Other patients can activate issues we may have with our own family. We can easily fall into the trap of trying to work out our concerns while attending to the patient's. We find ourselves so enmeshed in caregiving that we lose objectivity or perspective. We desperately want to help the patient because in doing so, we hope thereby to untangle our own internal confusion.

Listening to the dying takes us to the edge of our own fears, for when we open our hearts to someone, we open ourselves to their death.

Death will come in with a force equal to the resistance we have to it. The reaction we feel when confronting death is death confronting us. Our resistance comes from the tenacious hold we have on personal safety in the face of an event that represents the complete elimination of security. We are never on psychologically safe ground when we deal with death and dying. Our need for self-preservation can force us away from creative responses. We find ourselves responding with a cliché or saying something completely inappropriate.

We may approach the dying patient with a genuine desire to help but feel totally inadequate to do so. The truth is that we are inadequate at stemming the tide of a terminal illness. We do not need to force an answer to a problem that has no solution. We feel uncomfortable with not saying anything in the face of so much pain, so we endeavor to make death palatable by offering trite responses that frequently cause more difficulty than they solve. "It's God's will." "You need to get on with your life." "He's better off now." To the dying and the bereaved these phrases are confirmation that we are troubled by their pain but uninterested in them as individuals. Such comments are cues that there is no listening going on here at all. They are attempts to move away from our feelings of deficiency and the vulnerability of our own mortality.

If listening is to occur, it is imperative to become aware of our inner voice of protest. Only when we are unencumbered by our own history are we free to act spontaneously and appropriately within the context of the moment. One hospice nurse confided in me that, against everything she had learned in nursing school, she had once climbed in bed with a patient and snuggled next to her. It had felt like the appropriate response for this patient, who had voiced the fear of dying alone. The patient died half an hour later in the nurse's arms.

The more open and honest we are in facing our reactions, the less likely we are to rush in to fix situations without discovering what the patient actually wants. The more softly and gently we treat ourselves, the more available and compassionate we will be to those in need. We do unto others as we do unto ourselves. There are no demarcations between our inner psychic world and external circumstances except the ones we artificially impose.

The most difficult part of listening is learning to leave the other person alone. We try to apply our standards universally to resolve problems, but listening is not about problem solving. It is about the gift of our attention. Listening bestows on each individual her own uniqueness; free from our demands it fully acknowledges that person's worth by validating her. When we demand something from someone, we are requesting her to change or be altered. Listening does not demand anything; it allows everything to be just as it is. When a person is not pressured by the opinions of the listener, he no longer evaluates himself on external criteria and is therefore free to look within. Less external judgment frequently leads to less internal judgment and therefore to a natural growth of consciousness. With self-judgment temporarily abated, a person is able to move into areas within himself that call for his attention. He grows where he needs to grow merely by paying attention to those areas without aversion or criticism.

Growth has its own time frame. The patient's natural timing may make us impatient, but that is not the patient's problem. The listener moves at the speed of the patient, not the other way around. Through being heard we develop an inherent trust in our own growth process. Unburdened by criticism, a person's growth moves naturally toward greater openness. We become more at ease and have greater faith in the process of growing.

TRUE AND USEFUL

The Buddha stated clearly that saying only what is true is not sufficient for skillful speech. Speaking skillfully also requires saying what is useful for the listener to hear. One has to speak what is true and what is useful.

Honest feedback at first appears to be simply a matter of saying what is true, communicating what one actually sees as straightforwardly and reliably as one can. This, however, is not the full meaning. Viewing honest speech as simply a statement of fact leaves the impact of that fact out of consideration. Honesty needs to be tempered with timeliness. To tell someone that he is offensive in some way or other may be the truth, but it is an act of unkindness if that person is unprepared for such bluntness. Honesty without sensitivity can be a weapon.

To say what is true and useful involves the full-hearted sensitivity of the listener. When a hospice patient asks if he is going to die, the truth is, "Yes, of course, why else would you be in hospice care?" Usually that is far too coarse a response. A more appropriate answer might be, "What is your body telling you?" This allows the patient to come to his own truth through the experience of his body. For truth to have an impact on a person's growth it is necessary for the patient to hear it within the context of his own perceptions. If the timing is wrong, the patient's perceptions can cloud and twist the truth into something entirely different. If the truth is not useful, it will be distorted into a false perception.

Usefulness is the compassionate aspect of honesty. Truth can be a genuine gift or a weapon of destruction. It can cut and slice, or heal and mend. The determining factor is the context of the communication, which is as important as the truth of what is said. The context includes both when something is spoken and how it is said. The when and how of honesty allow the listener to grow from the feedback rather than recoil from it. This is the art of truthfulness.

The art of truthfulness can be applied to speech if the speaker first becomes aware of all the circumstances, both the external factors and the internal motivation for responding. Poor communication can occur if either one of these two cues is ignored. As long as our response includes an understanding of our own motivations, it will not come out of our own selfish needs. With full awareness of the external and internal cues of listening, our response flows from the situation itself without imposing an agenda. The wider the scope of our attention, the more love there will be in the reply. When our speech comes from a clear comprehension of the entire setting, our heart governs our communication. Attention is like a camera lens: the smaller the opening, the less light of understanding illumines the event; the wider the aperture, the better we see what is needed.

For example, it is impossible to be angry at someone and to understand the person at the same time. When we are angry our responses come from our self-righteousness. Our view is narrowed to our own opinion. To understand someone, we have to be willing to listen to that other person free from our perspective. This means that we have to expand our point of view to include the other's. Anger cannot sustain itself when we drop our self-righteousness.

I worked with Ellen, the hostile spouse of a patient close to death. She was deeply dependent upon her husband for almost every form of security. Poorly educated and illiterate, Ellen had left the responsibility for all their paperwork to her husband. He had not had time to teach her about these matters before he became too weak to do so. Feeling her vulnerability, Ellen railed at him and screamed at me. It was a house I enjoyed leaving. During one of my visits, Ellen happened to see an old photo of her husband. It depicted the two of them together, healthy and strong, on vacation. She started to tell me about their earlier life together. Her eyes softened, and she began to sob. Ellen went over, lay down beside him, and cried for a long time in his arms. Her anger could not continue in the face of the love she held for him.

INTIMACY

Most of us do not know how to die. It is not something we have rehearsed or practiced. We have a mind full of ideas about what will happen but little if any actual experience with the process. We need to have someone who knows, guides, teaches, and reassures us, someone we can trust, someone who will stand naked with us, who will not be overwhelmed. The dying need much more than pat answers or good feelings. Their hearts call for someone who can open into the unknown, someone who will travel the road of fear with them. To find such a companion is a very rare and precious occurrence.

Dying strips away everything that has kept us distant from each other. In this open vulnerability and shared pain there is little room to hide and nothing to protect. Our life as we have known it is essentially over. We have little need to defend ourselves. As Bob Dylan once sang, "When you got nothing, you got nothing to lose." From that void comes a willingness to expose ourselves to another.

Offering our attention during this time allows the dying companionship and a shared intimacy. Intimacy is the joining of human hearts allowing both participants to momentarily step out of their self-concern. People are more likely to live in isolation and die in company. We keep ourselves well protected until our time has run out. Then, in pain and with little to protect, we reach out for companionship.

As a hospice worker I was always astonished by the level of intimacy expressed to those of us who were strangers to the family. Almost all of the families welcomed us. They shared their quiet and heartrending stories in the most personal ways, allowing us to stand with them in the midst of their pain. The relationships seemed richer and more poignant because the usual formality of new acquaintances was eliminated. This raw trust brings out the best in us. Frequently, during the wake or funeral of the patient, a family member will rush past long-standing friends or relatives to hug and acknowledge the hospice worker. The hug symbolizes the level of human involvement during the death.

Most of us have known this level of intimacy only once or twice, perhaps when we first fell in love or when someone allowed us to share our pain with them. It is common to obtain this level of involvement when working with the dying. Over the years I have heard many hospice people attempt to describe what they receive from their work. Frequently they speak of how the families open their lives and how vulnerable and exposed they seem. A tenderness is communicated in these descriptions, a tenderness that indicates a high level of mutual respect and love.

Allowing ourselves to be vulnerable is not a display of weakness but of courage, the courage to meet someone in intimacy. The healing potential of the human heart is available only through intimacy. Reaching out with our listening, allowing others to expose their personal and family shadows, their grief and helplessness, their anger and fear, does not dull or dissolve these emotions. It simply provides a space for our human condition to be heard and acknowledged. When a person is able to stand in front of someone else and be granted permission to be just who he or she is, life meets life through the human heart. Life recognizes itself, and the effect of such a meeting is a gentle and joyous reunion.

The development of intimacy requires infinite patience and freedom from time constraints. There is no goal to the relationship. With goals, there are expectations and judgments all along the way. Patience requires no forethought of where the intimacy might take the speaker or the listener. It is an unguided journey deep into the hearts of both participants.

On several occasions, absorbed in intimate dialogue with a dying patient, I completely lost track of time. Often the patient and I would come out of that shared moment together and be amazed at the elapsed time. In the intimacy of that space there was no reference to time because neither of us were going anywhere. The feeling we came away with was that the moment was total and complete in itself. This was the result of both people dwelling together in their hearts.

The willingness to be intimate allows us to share the one thing we all value, genuine human warmth. Our time is their time, and we meet in the timeless. The speaker ingests the listener, and the listener, the speaker. Each of our roles becomes blurred, and it is no longer certain who is helping whom.

A spiritual teacher once said, "Love will not let us rest." The moments of love experienced through intimacy keep us working on ourselves so that we can abide for longer periods of time in that state. Initially at least, hospice workers associate this deep heartfelt contact with their work with the dying. The unknown and mysterious qualities of death keep us attentive, clear, and open in our relationship to the dying. The sadness is that we normally do not use the same quality of attention in all of our relationships. Many of us feel most alive when we are relating to death. Our other relationships seem to pale by comparison.

As many hospice workers come to eventually understand, these moments of openness are not dependent upon the dying at all. They are related to our ability to drop our own barriers and live free of fear. Hospice work is a tool with which we access our own potential. That potential is present in every relationship and in every moment. We can use our work with the dying as a portal through which we can step into universal intimacy. It takes a single step to walk over the threshold to love.

Listening and Speaking

Reflect upon what it means to understand someone. Think of a time when you were involved in an intimate conversation with another. Your heart was open and you both shared and listened with deep affection. What allowed you to understand the other person? What was the relationship between understanding and intimacy? Understanding and affection?

The next time you find yourself angry, be aware of how you listen to the other person's point of view. When you are angry, do you ever really listen to the other person? Now, in the midst of your anger, try to listen attentively and then see what effect your listening has on the anger. What does this teach you about listening and personal opinions?

Reflect on a meaningful and affectionate relationship that you have. What blocks you from listening to that person even more than you do now? Why are you only partially available? Reflect on what keeps you from participating fully and intimately.

Practice listening to a close friend or loved one without responding in any way. Do not give advice, opinions, or solutions. Do not judge or criticize this person or what he or she is saying. Watch your tendency to formulate a response rather than to listen. Be aware of nodding your head in agreement. Listen, through all your internal noise, to the other person's words and their impact on you. Connect with his or her pain or joy. How does your heart respond to this person's emotional life?

Reflect on your areas of prejudice. Where does prejudice still hide in your heart? Do you pretend to be tolerant even as you harbor intolerance? How does your prejudice manifest? Prejudice is hard to own if it does not fit your self-image. What part of your self-image feels betrayed by having this prejudice?

This exercise is difficult. The question to consider when approaching it is, Do you want to die with your prejudices or begin to understand them while you live? Merely thinking about them is not sufficient. You need to connect with them while they are active. If you can be aware of both your prejudice and the fear that drives it, you will make significant inroads toward understanding how and why it operates. Sit down and have a heartfelt conversation with someone about whom you harbor a prejudice. Watch how your mind wants to fix and hold that person in a predetermined way. Can listening occur in the middle of this projection, or are you constantly asserting your old ideas about who he is? Can you connect with the person's humanity? Can you access his pain? Are you able to own the anger that you project onto him? Accept the prejudice as coming from you and not as being true in itself. Owning your prejudice is the first step toward healing.

Reflect on a time when you were visiting someone who was very sick or dying and felt powerless to change the situation. Did you try to comfort the patient with false hope, or did you steer the conversation away from anything mean-ingful? Do you find yourself avoiding such situations, not knowing what to say? What is causing this reaction? What fears arise when you see someone dying?

Another difficult exercise. Intentionally seek out an opportunity to be with someone whose illness or infirmity causes you to feel uneasy. Can you be with both your reactions to the disease and the person at the same moment? Attempt to connect with the person and let the infirmity be just as it is. Work toward allowing the person and your reactions to be just as they are, without trying to change either one. See if you can listen through your reactivity without acting upon it. Try to bring the same quality of listening to your fear as you do to the person speaking.

Reflect on how sometimes you speak the truth but do so hurtfully. Is there a better way to say it? What else could you say that would allow others to hear your useful criticism? What are the limitations of just saying what is true?

Notice what occurs when you do not consider the usefulness of your speech. Are you in touch with your heart? How does the other person respond?

When you say something true without considering the other person's readiness to hear, you may do more harm than good. Practice giving feedback only when you include the other person's feelings within your response. Offer your feedback from genuine care and concern. What effect does this have on the other person's ability to hear?

8 | Searching for Meaning

People say that what we're all seeking is a meaning
for life. I don't think that's what we are seeking.
I think that what we're seeking is an experience of
being alive, so that our life experiences on the purely
physical plane will have resonances within our own
innermost being and reality, so that we actually feel
the rapture of being alive.
—JOSEPH CAMPBELL

ONE OF THE LESSONS we continually learn from the dying is that we are our own worst critics. Looking back across their lives as death approaches, the dying are often filled with overwhelming sadness and regret if their lives were not lived in accordance with their values. Others whose lives upheld their personal meaning usually meet death with more peace of mind. Some discover their purpose for living while they are dying. As we search for the purpose of life and grow in awareness, we each find meaning in our own terms. Whatever makes us come alive is what we value in life, and the importance of being authentic and living our values is brought home again and again as we observe the dying.

Every year we offer a session as part of our volunteer training where we ask the volunteers to choose the time frame of their own death. They are given three choices and asked to explain whichever choice they select. The choices are a quick death in which there is no warning or anticipation whatsoever, a death with a very short prognosis of only a few days, or a death with a prognosis between three and six months. Interestingly enough, each category usually receives about the same number of preferences. Explanations for each of the selections usually include remarks such as, for an unexpected death, "I do not want to go through the agony of knowing that I am going to die"; for a short prognosis, "I could do everything I wanted to do and say all my good-byes in a few days"; and, for a long prognosis, "I need time to put my affairs in order," or "I could tie up some loose ends and grow more intimate with my family if I had a few months."

Each of us places our own meaning and value on the time before death. For some, any amount of time in which we know we are going to die is too long. Having a terminal prognosis is seen as a burden on the family and emotionally draining on oneself. From this point of view dying depletes the family's resources and leads to a loss of control and stability. Dying, from this perspective, is an event to pass through as quickly as possible.

For others, dying is literally a once-in-a-lifetime opportunity. The possibilities available are limited only by the mental acuity of the dying mind. From this viewpoint dying is potentially an enriching experience for everyone involved. The difficulties are acknowledged, but they are seen in the context of the expectation of growth and intimacy for the whole family.

Usually people die after reaching a view somewhere between these two extremes. Often people who anticipate that dying will be an agonizing affair find something more significant within the experience than their fears allowed them to imagine. Conversely, those who believe the opportunities are endless often have very difficult moments, since dying can be a devastating experience for even the staunchest of hearts.

The meaning we give our death and dying is indicative of our psychic posture to life. It is derived from what we consider to be our purpose on earth, what we value and hold dear about being alive. When we face our death we look back across our life and evaluate it according to the meaning we ascribed to it. Usually we judge our own worth by how well we upheld this meaning. The outcome of that judgment is one of the indicators of how contentedly we will die.

I was a Buddhist monk with Jim, who had been an Australian fighter pilot during the Korean War. When he became a monk he had already decided that he would disrobe after only 278 days. He looked forward to ending his monk's life and would mark each day off his calendar. Since Jim was so anxious to depart, I asked him why he had ever decided to become a monk in the first place. He answered me with the following story.

During the Korean War a refugee boat left North Korea heading for the South. A South Korean military boat met the refugee boat to assist and aid the people on board. The refugee boat turned out to be a military decoy, blew itself up, and sank the South Korean boat that was alongside of it at the time. Two weeks later another boat left the North for the South claiming to have refugees on board. This time the South decided to sink the boat before it could blow itself up and cause damage to other boats in the area. The South ordered Jim, who was flying overhead, to destroy the boat. Jim did so. This time it turned out to be a refugee boat, not a military ploy, and 278 innocent people perished in the wreckage.

At first, Jim dismissed the carnage by telling himself war is war. Later, as he grew older, his values changed. Before he decided to take robes his guilt was so intense he could not live with himself another day. He became a monk to atone for those lost lives. Jim said that he was haunted by the fear of dying with this on his conscience.

If the actions we take are contrary to the meaning and purpose of our life, those actions can begin to obsess us with age. We set an internal standard, whose values are derived from our view of life's meaning, and hold ourselves accountable to preserving and maintaining that purpose throughout our living experience. But the meaning we give our lives can change with age, and what was once an acceptable activity can become prohibited. We can then judge our whole history with standards that we may have only recently acquired.

There is no single meaning that is true for all people at all times. There is no higher purpose or absolute significance that is inherent to life. Life is a blank slate on which we each write the meaning we choose. That meaning is forged by our interpretation of all the experiences that occur along the way. As Virginia Woolf wrote, "What is the meaning of life? ... The great revelation ... never did come. Instead there were little daily miracles, illuminations, matches struck unexpectedly in the dark."

HOPE

When we question the value and purpose of our lives we begin to assess who we are and where we are headed. These are the first stirrings from a heart that yearns to grow. Usually we begin asking these questions when we are in a crisis. When we lose a loved one or are confronted by death, we fall back and reflect, searching for answers that provide a context to make sense of these problems.

Who have I been all this time? How should I best fulfill my time on earth? These are spiritual questions that usually arise when we have witnessed the ending of our old attitudes, when the values we once held so dear are not sufficient to answer the devastation left by a loss. These questions arise from a search for something beyond the content of our personal suffering, for a meaning larger than ourselves, for a purpose that allows us to transcend the ordinary, the limited. If we can find such a purpose, our personal suffering is ennobled.

Most dying patients inquire into the value of their lives and the meaning their death holds. They plummet to the depths of their hearts, questioning their self-worth in the face of this pending adversity. Many go through a period of meaninglessness, despair, and hopelessness. Some contemplate, and a few commit, suicide. Out of this darkness many patients arrive at a new sense and purpose to life. They may reestablish values that have slipped away over the years or create new ones out of the ashes of circumstance.

Robert, a hospice patient, was a Texas truck driver and freewheeling spirit. He had driven tractor trailers for thirty years and had crisscrossed the country countless times. In the last few years following his retirement Robert had turned to his pickup truck to regain the freedom of the road. He spent most of his free time driving. He would go anywhere anytime and loved the feeling of the open road. He said he got his head in order while driving his truck.

Throughout the active outpatient treatment of his cancer Robert would drive for hours at a time while the chemotherapy infused into his arm. Now, as he became increasingly weak, it was obvious to everyone that he was a danger to himself and others on the road. The hospice nurse asked him to relinquish his keys. Robert said it was the hardest thing he ever had to do. For several weeks afterward he felt hopeless and despondent. He continued to sit in the cab of his stationary truck for long hours each day. Robert started to read the Bible in his cab as well. Slowly, over time, he stopped going out to his truck and would lie in bed just holding his Bible. The hospice chaplain worked with Robert until he died. Robert said he found new hope "in the word of God." He died with the Bible beside him, facing a window looking out onto his truck.

The focus of Robert's sense of hope and meaning had slowly changed over time. Although he was never completely able to let go of the symbolism of his truck, he was able to transfer new meaning and delight to his journey toward God. The new value he placed in the Bible absorbed some of the loss he felt around his inability to drive. Just being able to see his truck and hold his Bible seemed to infuse his spirit with renewed hope. Maybe he could still travel after all; maybe he felt free to begin this new journey.

We say in hospice work that, for the dying, the nature of hope changes from the hope of longevity to the hope of quality time. With this switch, hope becomes the process whereby patients begin to connect with their lives in an intimate way. They begin to live their aliveness rather than project their aliveness into future years. The patients begin to live their hope as an active expression of their purpose and meaning rather than postponing it until a later date. This urgency brings them face to face with their values. Often their actions unconsciously become more immediate, more personal, and more open. Frequently there is not as much forethought or hesitation. They begin to live the meaning they find rather than deliberate on it.

One way patients access their hope is in manifesting generosity, giving back to the world. Many dying patients make a tape of remembrance for their loved ones. Some work hard to complete a quilt or a final painting as their parting gift. Others decide to be part of a disease research project to give their illness meaning. Each small act of generosity extends their presence beyond their death. It moves them beyond their personal dilemma to the common base of humanity we all share.

This is a vital time in what Elisabeth Kübler-Ross calls "the final stage of growth." Hospice staff work hard to make this time useful and rich in whatever way the patient may direct it. Often there is a heightened sensitivity in the dying patient. He or she begins to receive the world of experience in more refined ways. The patient begins to notice parts of his life that were neglected in health. There is often a more subtle sense of beauty and appreciation. A patient may comment on the intricacies of a sunrise or sunset. She might hang up a bird feeder or fill her home with flowers. This may be the first time that the patient has found these experiences important. This joy and fullness of heart is another expression of quality time that gives the patient her parting sense of meaning and hope.

Sometimes the patient just wants to spend more time with his family. Quality time for this person might be to heal old wounds or relish the love that is present in a relationship. So much love can be expressed in such a short period of time. Often patients and spouses find their way back to the original meaning of their relationship with new heartfelt affection. Some renew their wedding vows on their deathbed. It is as if they had fallen in love all over again.

I worked with a couple who had been together over sixty years. Richard was dying and was confined to a wheelchair. He was attempting to protect Peg, his wife, from confronting the pain of his dying. He refused to speak to her about his illness. Peg would complain about Richard's lack of communication. Peg wanted nothing more than to share the journey with him. One day while I was speaking with Richard, he mentioned he wanted Peg to be with him when he died. I asked Richard if he had ever said that to Peg. He said he had not. I asked him if he would like to tell her now. He nodded, and I wheeled him out to where Peg was sitting. After stumbling around in speech for a while, he began to tell Peg how he wanted her by his side during his final moments. A floodgate of communication opened to the couple through that topic. A few days later I returned, and they were still sharing deeply together. They were shining and giddy. Richard pulled me aside and thanked me for giving him back his romance.

Many people come to the realization that love is the foundation upon which they give their lives meaning, even though love's motives are often disguised and subliminal. All the hours of work, the parenting, and even the arguments come down to the common denominator of love. Like Richard and Peg, people under the pressure of a time limitation can reunite in this common purpose and rediscover what has always been important.

Whether or not we find our true meaning to be love, there is still a search for purpose that goes on in almost everyone. We all search for a context to validate ourselves. Once we discover it, we can then commit our energy and resources, and it will carry over into everything we do.

I recently heard a radio interview with a chef renowned for his excellent barbecued ribs. The interviewer asked him what combination of factors made his meat special. The chef talked about the seasonings and the construction of the barbecue pit. He hesitated and then said that while he was working with these ingredients he pictured his children. This was his secret recipe. The meaning that gave this man his purpose was love. He imparted the special ingredient of love for his children into each meal.

Meaning has fulfillment only in action, in our ability to live out our values. The usual way meaning translates into action is through an applied belief. It is something we think about and then do. We have not integrated it sufficiently for it to be spontaneous. We attempt to align ourselves with our purpose, but it always feels a little pretentious, as if we are trying on an oversized coat. When we are dying, we may cast aside the coat altogether. We have no time to spend in the dressing room; we throw ourselves into the immediacy of our aliveness. If we have spent sufficient time in the past mulling over and working on these values, we are more apt to access them spontaneously when our lives depend on it.

I was recently involved in a management meeting that was several months in planning. A number of people were arriving from another city to attend, and fixing a date that was convenient for all the participants had been difficult. In the middle of the meeting a hospice nurse called informing me that a personal friend of mine under our hospice care was actively dying and had requested I come. I went up to my boss, who was also attending the meeting, and told him I needed to leave.

He tried to dissuade me. I did not even listen to his argument because the value I placed on attending my friend's death was much stronger than my need to keep my job. I did not even think about it. There was no choice. I just got up, excused myself, and left.

During such moments of clarity, meaning ends. Meaning dissolves into action and is no longer a factor in our decisions. These moments indicate that we have completely assimilated the meaning, and it no longer stands as an ethical issue through which we screen our responses. In some mysterious way we have transformed all our deliberations into an integrated whole action.

Another way that a patient expresses hope for quality time is through his attitude toward dying. How does he face death? What does he rely on to give these circumstances meaning? In the years of my hospice work I have seen countless patients struggle with these issues.

Patients will often go through a process called "life review" in an attempt to come to terms with this issue. The dying will frequently want to process parts of their lives that are emotionally charged or ambiguous. They want to talk through and replay areas where they feel stuck or frozen, in hopes of reaching some kind of settlement within themselves, a summation of worth and value. A patient's attitude toward dying is partially determined by the outcome of this process.

The patient will usually direct the hospice worker in this life review. The hospice worker needs to do very little except to create an atmosphere where the patient does not feel any judgment, regardless of what is disclosed. As the following story suggests, this process can be as difficult for the listener as for the patient.

After extended life review sessions Janice concluded that she needed to atone for all her sins. The hospice social worker called in the hospice chaplain to help Janice work through this process. Janice began refusing her pain medication. She believed that through her physical pain she would cleanse her soul and align herself with God. She said the experience of pain brought her closer to Christ because it helped her appreciate his suffering. The chaplain was dismayed. From the chaplain's perspective there were no overriding issues in Janice's life. She had lived a very human life with the normal number of problems and disappointments. Regardless of the chaplain's intervention, Janice steadfastly refused her medicines. Her pain was noticeably increasing. At one point the chaplain asked Janice how she would know when she had suffered enough. The patient responded, "When I die, I will have suffered enough."

Janice's case demonstrates the quandary in which hospice caregivers often find themselves. Our work is to help the patient find her own meaning, her own quality of life, and ultimately her own freedom. This means letting go of our authority over events and procedures. While we work diligently to make sure that a person's decisions are based on clear understanding, ultimately it is the patient and her family who decide among the options presented. In this case, the hospice staff had to witness Janice die in physical torment without interfering.

Janice, believing that suffering would absolve her sins and thereby earn her forgiveness, had decided to force herself to suffer. She found spiritual value in her pain. As difficult as this may be for us to watch, it is through living out her convictions that the patient feels validated and aligned with her purpose and meaning. Hope for Janice meant living out her spiritual values in the way she defined them.

Hope is fulfilled when we sustain our purpose for living and maintain our personal meaning through adversity. When we have been stripped of any chance for a cure, our expectation shifts to having a meaningful death, a death with quality. Many dying patients struggle with meaning because their life is not working. Those who die peacefully usually have their life in order and working to their satisfaction. They experience no separation between their life and their values. They do not strive for meaning because they are living their meaning every day. If we wish to give hope and be of help to the dying, we can do so by allowing them to die their own deaths, within their own framework of meaning. This becomes most people's definition of a good death.

THE RELATIVITY OF MEANING

The meaning we give our actions and the value we assign our lives are determined by how we understand our place in the world. This understanding changes constantly moment after moment depending on circumstances. We usually have one perception of our value as a wife, another as a mother, a third as a supervisor, and so on. It also fluctuates based on what we are called to do, the emotion we are feeling, and the circumstances. Most of us are familiar with feeling good about ourselves one moment and self-critical the next. What we usually miss, as these perceptions shift, is how our worldview also changes. As our self-understanding varies, so too does the meaning and value we place on the world. The meaning that life holds for us depends upon how we happen to define ourselves in the moment.

Self-understanding and meaning are not static, isolated perceptions; they are interwoven. We like to think of our psychic posture as constant and consistent, but this is not the case. When we look closely we see that the sense of who we are changes with our circumstances and surroundings. For example, during our more reactive moments we feel constricted, isolated, and self-enclosed. But, at other times, such as when we are in nature, we may feel a great deal of inward space and freedom. We move back and forth along a continuum between these larger and smaller senses of self throughout the day.

Sometimes an unusual event can move us off this continuum, forcing a redefinition of ourselves. Facing one's death, a loss of a loved one, or a moment of severe trauma can dramatically shake our self-perceptions. Events such as these can potentially shut down our defensive mechanisms, which usually protect us from feeling overwhelmed by a more expansive consciousness without boundaries. These events can shatter our normal understanding of the world order and awaken us to the presence of something bigger than ourselves. Once this perspective is seen, it can completely change the meaning we give our lives and the purpose we play in the world.

My brother spent almost twenty years addicted to narcotics. For most of that time he lived in rather squalid conditions in Chicago. One night an obviously intoxicated man broke into his apartment and demanded drugs, which he knew my brother usually had available. On this particular occasion my brother did not have any narcotics in his apartment. The intruder did not believe him and placed a gun next to his head demanding that my brother produce the drugs. After repeated denials the man pulled the trigger, but the gun did not go off. Cursing at the gun, he pointed it again at my brother's head, pulled the trigger, and yet again the gun did not go off. Frustrated, the man left the apartment. From his window, my brother watched him walk outside, raise the same pistol into the air, and pull the trigger. The gun fired.

My brother said he changed in that instant. He quickly gave up drugs and became a rather fervent Christian. He said that incident caused a shift in his perception of the world and his place in it. The world and his sense of self blended into something much bigger than either one alone. In that moment he knew he had never been the isolated person he had always believed himself to be. He talked about the obvious unity of all life. Since then, he has been living his life with very different priorities and a renewed connection to the world.

Experiences such as my brother's can transform our sense of self, expanding it to encompass wider aspects of the world. At such times we feel less defined by the mind and body and more in harmony with the universe. But such transformations are not permanent. The nature of life is change, and, under different circumstances, we again find ourselves in situations that give rise to fear and reactivity. As our world view narrows and life is seen in terms of self and other, we once again focus on self-preservation.

An expansive and encompassing perception of the world is not hypothetical; it is no less objective and observable than the view in which we currently participate. We always see from one vantage point or another, and each perspective has its own truth, but the truths of the more inclusive levels are inaccessible when we are lost in self-preservation.

At the most restrictive level, the self is defined by the contents of the mind. Usually there is a strongly held belief in selfhood: in a fixed and static entity who controls events. Everything outside the mind, and even the shadowed parts within it, are a potential threat to the organism. A person's view from this perspective can be either theistic or atheistic. Either way, the world is very linear and delineated and understood in terms of self-protection and accumulation. People and situations are perceived as either working for or against oneself, and actions are usually undertaken in response to pleasure and pain. Since we see the world as a separate and distant object, we are constantly concerned with bringing objects into our sphere of influence. We may also depend on strong defense mechanisms to keep perceived threats at bay. Gain and loss are our standard measures of success or failure. Death is viewed in strict contrast to life; life is a treasure to acquire, and death the ultimate loss.

The opposite understanding is that of the all-inclusive self. Since objects are not felt as a limitation or a hindrance to happiness, great joy can arise. Contentment comes from being with life as it is, not from gaining advantages or avoiding situations. Everything that obstructs this contentment is perceived as an opportunity for growth rather than a threat to our security. No division is created between life and death. The sense of "I" expands beyond the boundaries of our skin and individual mind. Everything becomes part of us. We have a sense of spaciousness, much affection for others, and little need to protect or defend what we do. Through our actions, we seek to realign ourselves with the intention of our hearts. Compassionate action, based on a generosity of spirit, is the way we serve the world. There is joyful service with little burnout or depletion.

We have all experienced such all-embracing inclusiveness in our lives. Many people, especially during childhood, have felt the joy of an expansive unity. Conversely, we all remember times when we were so caught in our own pain and self-concern that there was no room in our hearts for anyone. What is important in one moment evolves into something very different in the next. We move between the extremes of openhearted love and closed-minded self-preservation. Yet we usually define our self-image as a specific point along the continuum and disregard those moments when we are either more expansive or more contracted. We hold ourselves as fixed when we are actually fluid. We say, "I am this way; this is who I am." We keep repositioning ourselves as who we believe ourselves to be, not who we actually are.

When psychedelic drugs were the rage back in the sixties many people were able to use them to relax their self-identifying patterns. When they came down from the drug, however, they were back with their old meaning and views. They did not perceive the relativity of the states they were experiencing and kept attempting to reinstate and maintain them. But shifts of understanding occur throughout our life, even though we seldom acknowledge them. Some shifts may be so shattering to our self-image that we consciously suppress them. Mostly, however, we just ignore them as irrelevant.

Art is a friend of mine who is dying of AIDS. He is an extraordinary man full of passion and wisdom, which he attributes both to a life of self-awareness and to his terminal illness. He has written a book on his illness and the truths that he garners from his pending death. I have been present when Art is teaching, and he speaks from great depth and clarity. In casual conversation he often moves beyond himself in both his view and perception. There can be a pervasive sense of universal understanding and spaciousness in Art's actions and speech.

Not long ago I called to check on how Art was doing. He had a temperature of 105 degrees and had just been discharged from the hospital. He was miserable and in a self-protective mood. He wanted to limit all human contacts and remain alone. He refused a book tour and all teaching engagements for the entire year. Art was turning inward and only wanted to be around his closest friends. He seemed a little angry and irritable as we spoke.

I asked him about these changes. Art saw no contradiction in these two contrasting psychic postures. He said that sometimes the AIDS touched off his deepest fears and all he wanted to do was escape. He saw no value in being sick and would do anything to eliminate the disease. At other times, he said, he would speak to his illness like a friend, giving it a name and treating it as a part of himself. He would bargain, cajole, and engage his illness as a playmate. Occasionally during these moments he was unaware that he was sick at all. He would relate to death as just another moment of life.

There was no contradiction in Art because he was not identifying with one of these views at the expense of the others. He was not trying to return to the more spacious perception or fight against his fear. He remained accepting of both his fear and his joy. His meaning and purpose altered depending on his perspective, and he would act from whatever seemed true to him in that moment. If that meant canceling a prearranged book signing tour, so be it. What was important to him was his immediate understanding, not his adherence to a consistent self-image.

All of our views, from selfishness to oneness, are relative. They are single slices of a pie. Real freedom is not located within any one view. The more expansive perceptions allow us more inward freedom and less personal suffering, but they are relative views nevertheless. When we believe in one perspective over and above the others, we feel the suffering associated with that view. Since we can learn a great deal from all views, we would do well to refuse to rely on any single one to determine our identity or our reality. We are then free to dance among the many meanings that life has to offer.

Finding Meaning

Reflect on different time frames for your death. Consider alternatives including an immediate death, a short prognosis of a few days, or a prognosis of three to six months. Put yourself in each of the three scenarios. What are the advantages and disadvantages of each? Reflect on the value of the time before you die. What would make that time meaningful? What would make it difficult?

Choose one of the three time frames for your death. Pretend you know how long you are going to live. Practice living a full day with that prognosis. Do every act during the day with the time frame of your death in mind. How are you using the time remaining? Are you doing anything differently? After living this day become aware of how you may be living your life at the expense of the things you hold most dear.

Reflect on what gives your life meaning. What sustains you through difficult times? If the time had come for you to die, what would give you strength? Would it be people, your values, your sense of self-worth? What happens to these things when you forget your death?

Make a list of your current priorities and study each one. Think about which values you feel would be important if you were close to death and reviewing your life. Is your list of priorities in agreement or in contention with your lifelong values? Watch your activities for one week, and see if your long-term values are aligned with how you live your life from day to day.

Reflect on the relativity of the meaning of your life. Have there been moments in your life when you felt the presence of something larger than yourself? How did you relate to these moments? Was there interest, fear, or indifference? Did the meaning you give your life change after these experiences? In what way and for how long?

How does the way you define yourself affect what you value and find meaningful? Notice in the course of a day how you reshuffle your values as you react to different events and situations. When you are hungry or angry, how do your values change? Do your moods drive your purpose? Do you hold core values that you consider primary? Determine in the morning what is meaningful to you on this particular day. In the evening see if the same meaning has remained constant or altered.

9 | Understanding Our Suffering

Long have you suffered the deaths of fathers and
mothers and sons and daughters, brothers and sisters,
and while you have thus suffered, you have shed more
tears upon this long way than there is water in the four
great oceans. And, thus, have you long undergone
suffering . . . and filled the graveyards full.
—BUDDHA

WHEN WE COMMIT OURSELVES to learning about life, we become increasingly sensitive to the motivations behind our actions. We begin to accept responsibility for the role we play in our conflicts and reactions. To understand and transcend our suffering is the purpose of a spiritual journey. We rarely appreciate the lessons suffering can impart because we spend so much time trying to avoid the pain. The little deaths that touch our lives—the ending of a relationship, a fading dream, a lost hope, the daily disappointments—take their toll in mental anguish. These small indicators are wake up calls to pay attention. Then, when physical death does arrive, we will have a conditioned readiness to fully explore our relationship to it.

It is said that upon leaving the safety of the castle walls that had protected him from any semblance of suffering during his youth, Prince Siddhartha witnessed the old, the sick, and the dying for the first time in his life. He was so moved by the suffering of others that he vowed to find a way to end the sorrow of existence. Through his search he became the Buddha and pointed the way out of suffering for all who would listen.

In the West the search for the Fountain of Youth was really this same longing. It was an attempt to end the suffering of old age and death. Unlike the Buddha, seekers after the Fountain of Youth wanted to stay forever young. The Buddha wanted to understand why and how we suffer.

Scientists are currently striving to solve the genetic puzzle of the aging process in an attempt to ward off the suffering that is inevitable with old age. Many people believe that this is one of the greatest issues confronting human beings. If we could solve the problem of aging, we would be moving the world closer to a utopia.

But is that so? How many of us would choose to drink from the Fountain of Youth? What would the world be like if death did not exist? As one Zen master said, "We should be happy that we will die. If we lived forever, we would have a real problem." From one perspective death can be seen as both a problem and a solution. We cannot live with it, and we cannot live without it. From another view the problem has never been old age, sickness, or death. The problem is not what we suffer from but why we suffer at all.

There is an immeasurable amount of suffering in this world. It seems vast and infinite in its variations and disguises, from the obvious litany of war, famine, and plague to the subtle self-induced forms, such as unworthiness, lack of self-forgiveness, and loneliness. Think for a moment of the pain and tragedy that befalls each of us in the course of a single lifetime. Reflect on the jilted hearts, the broken bones, the traumatic losses, the disappointments. Now multiply this times the number of people on the earth, and we have only scraped the surface of the endless sorrow of humankind.

The universality of suffering is brought home to each one of us in different ways. I remember as a monk in Asia living in a small monastery on an island off the coast of Thailand. I had been staying there for several months. Each morning I would walk along the beach toward a small village on my way to alms rounds. The beauty of the sunrise was always striking at this time of morning, and I would enjoy my solitary walk. One morning I saw a distant shape on the beach that I could not identify. There was a village fisherman standing alongside the object. As I approached I saw it was a human corpse that had been in the sea for so long it was unrecognizable as a human body except for its head. The fisherman guessed that it was a Vietnamese boat person who had died at sea and floated onto the shore. He conjectured that the boat had probably been overrun by pirates, who were prevalent at that time off Thailand's coast.

Here I was, thoroughly enjoying the morning sunrise in one moment and deeply moved over this tragedy in the next. The stark contrast between the utter simplicity of my life as a monk and this corpse washed up on the beach remains with me to this day. This surreal image spoke to me of the immensity of suffering in all of its forms.

Suffering is not the only component to life, but it can easily intrude upon any aspect of our experience in any given moment. It is unpredictable. It keeps us on guard and suspicious when everything is going well. We want to keep looking over our shoulder and checking things out. Can I really be this happy? Situations inevitably do change and we fall back to the feared reality of our pain.

We feel out of control when we are suffering. Like a small boat on the ocean we are at the mercy of circumstances beyond our command. The weather changes, and suddenly we are caught in a storm. In the middle of the high waves we lose perspective. It seems like the storm will never end. It appears that there is nothing we can do to regain our happiness. It becomes difficult to trust life when it is so out of our control.

Suffering can rob us of our meaning and hope. It can lead us into dark regions of despair where the world seems capricious and where our self-esteem erodes away. Suffering becomes the bane of our existence as we try in vain to keep it from arising. We can tolerate a little as long as it is interspersed with enough pleasure, but when pain becomes too intense and persistent, life is no longer worth living.

Many hospice families console themselves after the death of a loved one by saying that they are glad the patient died when he did because now he will no longer have to suffer. Often the death went smoothly and there was not a great deal of distress, but if the family believes he was in pain, it makes it that much easier to let him go. If a person is suffering, his life must not be worth living. The usual message of a concerned family is "Anything but suffering."

Suffering, however, can trick us into identifying with it so that we subtly encourage its continuance. We become so accustomed to our depression that we go home each night, close the shades, put a sad song on our tape deck, and bathe ourselves in our melancholy. We are comfortable with our depression because it is familiar; there are no surprises even as we succumb to the heaviness of the mood. Our suffering can become so ordinary, we forget who we are without it.

The question is, are we willing to give it up? Are we willing, without a guarantee of any substituted happiness, to let go of it completely? It does not seem possible to find our way out of the entanglement of our suffering unless we are willing to learn from it. It is a contradiction to want to learn from our pain and encourage its continuance in the same moment.

When the young Siddhartha ventured out from his fortress of safety, he was making a statement about what is necessary to end a life of suffering. He was saying that there is something more profound than our desire for the security and pleasure of a princely life. Our desire for happiness pushes us into a single-minded pursuit of pleasure and avoidance of pain. We are unable to understand suffering fully until we allow ourselves to feel its effects and investigate its cause. The Buddha's secret will remain hidden until each of us risks losing our own forms of princely life.

UNDERSTANDING SUFFERING

The urge to learn pulls us ever deeper into ourselves. We become increasingly able to hear the reasons why we do the things we do. We have ignored our suffering for so long that we rarely appreciate the learning that pain can impart. Sometimes we must be dragged through great hardship to access the answers. Like the warning lights on the dashboard of the car, mental agitation, fear, and anxiety alert us to our deep-seated problems. We can use these mental reactions to uncover the sources of our pain, but first we have to interpret them correctly. We must penetrate and decipher their codes, render them discernible. Usually we are so aversive to pain, however, we will do anything to cast it out of our lives. We want to get rid of it, not understand it.

Sometimes we unskillfully use pain to reinforce our positions in life.

"I know she won't like me" and "Why even try? I can't do it" are two of the many self-defeating expressions that arise from our history with pain. We anticipate the future to be as cruel as the past and therefore shy away from whatever new is coming our way. Imprisoned in our old painful self-image, we see our suffering as proof that we are undeserving; we use it to justify our unworthiness, unattractiveness, or some other inadequacy.

We often treat pain as a personal burden that the universe is forcing on us rather than seeing the impersonal lessons that pain contains. Pain is impersonal because it is transpersonally true. We all suffer for the same reasons. The content of our suffering is different for each individual, but the fundamental cause of the pain is common to us all. If we are able to put a little space between ourselves and our tendency to blame, we would see a universal message about the nature of suffering. When we assert our own justification for our distress, we tend to miss the common thread.

The different ways we explain our suffering reflect our understandings of the world. A life-threatening illness can open us to a subtle level of understanding because our usual explanations of pain become insufficient. It is difficult to blame the reality of death on anyone. Death takes us beyond our accusations to our collective heritage.

The mother of a friend of mine was in critical condition for a number of weeks after an automobile accident. My friend was very interested in exploring with his mother the enormous suffering that arose from this misfortune. He would sit and investigate with her the relationship of her mind to her body. He said they went to very deep places together. His mother would come out of these meditations with a clear understanding of the impersonal nature of the pain. She would speak about feeling connected with all people who were suffering. She began to relate to the common shared pain of all humanity.

A few weeks later she was no longer in critical condition, and much of her physical pain had abated. Once she was on the road to recovery, however, she was no longer interested in self-discovery and refused to speak to her son about any of that "New Age stuff." Once the motivating force of her self-inquiry had been removed, her old habit patterns reemerged. Instead she became angry at the motorist who caused the accident and planned a lawsuit.

Our usual level of understanding pain is to look outside ourselves for explanations. We point fingers so we do not have to assume responsibility for our difficulty. We use expressions like "You make me angry" to ward off accountability for our suffering. Our tendency is to become self-defensive and deflect the issue away from ourselves.

But it does not make sense to blame ourselves either. Making mistakes is a part of being alive. We are not the masters of our destiny, and it is simply beyond our ability to control much of life. We have the idea that if we had just tried harder or had altered our route a little, our problems would not exist. We find ourselves always looking back, holding ourselves accountable for the chaos and change of an uncertain universe.

One way we strive to maintain our innocence is to blame our suffering on the content of our lives: on events, persons, scenarios. These circumstances become the focus for our wrath. "If only it had not rained today." "If only we had a bigger house." "If only I had another job." But the content actually has nothing to do with the source of our anxiety. The content is simply the unfolding of events that are usually beyond our control. Sometimes those events are pleasant, sometimes unpleasant.

We are missing the point when we blame either ourselves or the content of our lives for our suffering. We can take responsibility for causing our suffering without accepting personal blame. The way to begin is to look at our relationship to what we see as the cause of our suffering. How are we relating to the problem—our illness, our broken leg, our lost lover? When we take responsibility for this relationship, we assume accountability for the one component of life that we can affect: our responses. We begin to make life more workable by interceding between the pain and our fear or aversion to it.

Harvard University conducted a study with a group of meditation students in the 1980s. The study was to determine the effects of pain on meditation students after a prolonged period of silent practice.

This particular style of meditation emphasized cultivating a moment-to-moment awareness of the mind and body process. Before and after an intensive three-month retreat, each student was given a test by submerging his or her hand in ice water for a few minutes and reporting both the physical pain and the mental suffering associated with the cold. There was a significant difference between the scores before and after the course. Although the value reported for the physical pain stayed about the same before and after the retreat, the mental reaction to the pain decreased significantly. In other words the retreatants were still feeling the same physical discomfort but were suffering less.

At some point we all have physical pain. How our mind relates to it determines how much agony we will feel. If we react with stress, tension, fear, and agitation, our suffering will increase. The prolonged meditation course gave the retreatants the psychic space to accommodate the pain with little reaction. Through meditation they learned to understand and accommodate their reactivity. In facing their fear directly, the retreatants weakened the link between pain and anxiety and thereby diminished their mental suffering significantly.

Daniel, an elderly man, had prostate cancer with tumors that had spread to his spine. The hospice tried in vain to alleviate Daniel's intense pain, for Daniel refused to take any medicines that would alter his clarity or sedate him. Out of frustration the hospice nurse called in a meditation teacher as a consultant to work with Daniel on his anxiety and fear surrounding his pain. The meditation teacher had Daniel become aware of the sensations of pain without pulling back in aversion or fear. He asked Daniel simply to notice what the sensations felt like and allow them to be present within his consciousness. After several sessions Daniel was markedly more relaxed and at ease with his pain, even though he said the pain itself had not diminished.

We can substitute any aspect of our lives, and the same rule applies. If we lose our partner, become ill, or our house burns down, it is all part of the ever-changing content of our lives. No matter what we do, our influence over the content is limited. We can greatly affect the degree of our suffering, however, when we understand how our mental reactions affect our relationship to the content. The only control we have is over our reactivity, and that is all we need to live a life of diminished suffering.

IN CONFLICT WITH REALITY

Suffering is a call for attention. It signals an area of ourselves that is out of alignment, a mental process needing adjustment. We suffer when life goes one way and our minds go another, when we want X to happen and Y is the reality. The emergence of a strong desire or fear relative to an existing predicament will usually mean we are suffering. The mind attempts to formulate its own reality to replace the current unpleasant circumstances. It creates its own mental fiction and then lives from that illusion at the expense of what is true.

The truth of course is that our mental desire is only a wish, and when the wish is in conflict with what is true, we suffer. We may live with such strong attachment to our mental fabrications that reality takes on a secondary significance to what we want. It is as if we play God and create our own world view, and when this view is shattered by reality, we wonder why life is so tragic. Life has always been just the way it is. The tragedy comes from denying the truth of the actual and trying to control it by mentally rearranging the facts before our eyes.

Eventually the friction between these two becomes unbearable, the suffering too immense to continue to play make-believe. We would rather continue following our desires, but at some point we can no longer live at the expense of what is really happening. At first we try to improve the content so that it matches our desire. We adjust our living situations, find a new mate, or change jobs. Since our desires are endless and all content eventually changes into something we no longer want, this strategy proves to be unsuccessful.

Next we attempt to polish the self. We may try all forms of self-improvement to live more comfortably with our stress and anxiety. We find that our suffering continues, however, because these forms usually arise out of another desire: to be different than we are. This puts us back in conflict with reality, and the problem continues.

Eventually, however, we find ourselves penned in. We cannot change the content, nor can we change ourselves to successfully eliminate our suffering. We are forced to acquiesce to what reality is offering. This process leads us through the stages of loss. We grieve the life we cannot have. This grief slowly moves the mind from denial to acceptance. We drop our resistances and finally allow life to show itself in all of its tragic and comic manifestations.

We all have areas where we cannot let go of our suffering. Some of us suffer the most in relationship to our physical body, for others emotions entangle them in intense pain. Moment after moment we move up or down the scale of suffering. Sometimes we complain and point fingers, while at other times we are centered and intent on learning from our distress.

When Christ was dying on the cross, it is said, he called out, "Why have you forsaken me?" This may not be any different than a hospice patient asking, "Why is God doing this to me?" Every mind seems capable of slipping in its range of understanding. Every mind seems to move back and forth on the continuum of grasping and letting go.

As we align ourselves with what life actually offers as opposed to how we wish it to be, the meaning of suffering begins to evolve. This becomes apparent in many of our hospice patients as they move from self-inflicted punishment to an understanding of the impersonal causes of their suffering. Many of them learn an enormous amount about this whole process in a very short period of time because death refuses to let them compromise. They are forced to understand their suffering because they are unable to bargain their way out of it. They are unable to move away to another topic for very long. There is simply nowhere to go.

Our hospice team was involved with Alma, a fifty-two-year-old woman who was dying of liver cancer. Alma had lived a hard life and held many regrets. She felt guilty about a history of neglect of her children. As she attempted to come to terms with her psychological pain, she initially related to her physical discomfort as an opportunity to punish herself for her years of unavailability. In her stoicism she would deny she was suffering at all. The nurse said her pain became so intense that at times Alma seemed unable to speak for fear of crying out in agony. The social worker spent several sessions working with Alma's need to suffer. She showed Alma that noncompliance with her medication regime was causing her family more stress, and she was hurting the very people she was trying to appease. When Alma realized this fact she started to take her medications.

The social worker and the chaplain spent several more weeks working with Alma on her self-forgiveness. The chaplain said she never saw anyone more motivated to learn and forgive. Alma seemed truly to come to terms with her self-blame. In the last week of her life, her mind appeared to be spacious and accommodating. She no longer showed any signs of self-abuse, and she seemed filled with affection for others. Although her family was unable to move as far in their forgiveness of Alma as Alma did in her self-forgiveness, she seemed to understand that as well.

There is an opportunity at death to give up all self-images, positive or negative. For people who have a low sense of self-worth, negative qualities can be more tenacious than positive ones because we believe in them more strongly. We often believe that we deserve to suffer, given how badly we feel about ourselves. We can even feel guilty for being happy. When we understand how persistent a sense of unworthiness can be, examples like Alma—who succeeded in working through her negative self-images and dying with clarity—are all the more striking.

When the body is close to death there is no longer a great need to protect our reputation or self-images. We can risk changing. We can become a little easier on ourselves, less tied to the conditioned scripts of our past. This absence of tension allows us to be more objective about ourselves and not quite so demanding. Although Alma's degree of healing is rare, this potential growth is available to all of us throughout life.

Once freed from the images and life scripts, we become less bound by the content of our lives. We begin to see things in perspective with a little less judgment and criticism. We have more affection for others and focus less on ourselves. Often an appreciation arises around the fluidity and changing nature of life. A more stable contentment develops, one that does not depend upon our emotional or physical environment.

True contentment does not deny states of mind like joy and happiness or anger and sorrow. Nor does it rest upon them as being complete in themselves. How can we rest upon any state of mind for fulfillment when all states, by their very nature, must die? Joy and happiness do not last. Death shows us what authentic contentment is because it eventually eliminates everything that is not real. What is left after death is what is true.

Suffering is an indication that we are binding ourselves to something that must inevitably die. We can ride the waves of change for a while, but the waves eventually crash onto the shore. When Christ said, "Do not lay up your treasures where rust corrupts or thieves get in," he seemed to be addressing this point about suffering.

Death can teach us to differentiate between true contentment and the transitory forms of happiness. It focuses our attention on the changing nature of this world in which everything continually evolves into new shapes and forms. Whatever is temporary and finite must eventually lead to disappointment and pain because it cannot sustain itself over time. What we once loved withers and dies; what we once found pleasurable is now empty and dry. Everything is evolving into something other than what it was. Pleasure passes into pain, and we are left grieving.

The question that death poses is, What lies beyond? Beyond our suffering? Beyond change? Is there a truth that does not rely on unstable conditions for its contentment? Our pursuit of learning in the face of death exposes us to the answer that satisfies these questions and leads us beyond death itself.

Befriending Pain

Reflect on the personal pain in your life. Consider the subtle as well as the obvious forms of your mental and physical suffering. Include your difficult emotions and your self-criticism. Think about situations and circumstances that generate suffering. How much of it do you inflict on yourself, and how much do you blame on others? Reflect on how you attempt to control the situations that lead you to suffer. How much of it is controllable, and how much is beyond your influence?

Be aware of all the different expressions of your suffering for one week. Use the week to focus on the gross and subtle forms of your personal pain as it occurs throughout the day. Each time you find yourself in pain, ask yourself: Who is responsible for this pain? Watch your tendency to blame and externalize the causes. Become aware of your need to be in control of your happiness, and see how suffering seems to intrude on your plans. Experience situations in which you clearly have no control. What feelings arise? What is the relationship between suffering and control?

Reflect on the difference between pain and suffering. These two can easily become enmeshed and indistinct. There is physical pain and your reaction to it, emotional difficulty and your discomfort with it, the sensation of pain and your reaction of suffering. Reflect on how much of your anguish is caused by your reaction to pain as opposed to the unpleasantness of the pain itself.

Take the next opportunity you have to experience painful sensations and suffering as two separate events. Reacting to an unpleasant sensation is suffering. Separate the sensation from the suffering. For example, suppose you hurt your knee or burn your finger. Experience the physical pain as an unpleasant sensation. Notice how much fear, condemnation, and anger are caused by reacting to that pain. Is it possible to accommodate these reactions without letting them spin you out of control? What happens to the intensity of the pain when you are able to let go of the reactivity?

Reflect on the impersonal quality of pain. Is there anyone who does not experience pain at one time or another? Given that a certain amount of pain in your life is inevitable, how do you handle it? Can you take responsibility for your allotment? How much bitterness do you carry for your share of universal pain?

The next time you are in pain, attempt to experience it as just sensation. Try not to see it as your pain but only as sensations without an owner. You can act on the pain appropriately without being fearful or identifying it as yours. Notice the link between the sensations and the identification and ownership of the pain. Watch how the mind elaborates on these sensations to make them more than what they are. You go from a simple burn to fear of having inflicted real damage, to infection and disfigurement. This is how fear elevates pain beyond reasonable limits into mental agitation.

Reflect on the nature of desire and fear. How do desire and fear project their own reality? Think about what a desire is. Does it have any reality other than a mental wish? How much of your activity is forged around wish fulfillment as opposed to accommodating things as they are?

To experience the relationship between desire and suffering, focus on any situation in which you want to have something or want something to happen. In the middle of that desire, can you settle with the situation as it is, or are you forced to play out what your mind tells you it wants? See the choices before you. You can accept what reality is offering, or you can pursue your imagination. Play with a desire, sometimes indulging and sometimes holding back. Learn all about the nature of desire as it pulls your mind away from reality toward an imaginary future.

10 | Opening Our Hearts

*The receptive quality of love allows every experience
to enter us, to touch us. It allows us to be touched by
the wind and the sun, by other people, and by each
part of ourselves, by the trees, the birds, and all of
nature. [It] is the practice of intimacy with all of life.*
—JOSEPH GOLDSTEIN

AS WE BEGIN TO UNDERSTAND our own suffering, we
become more aware of the degree of suffering in others. This perception opens our heart to compassion and love. We begin to genuinely
care about the welfare of others. This is not a superficial or self-serving
love; it flows from the heart when we experience how connected we
are to others.

There is so much confusion about love. Nothing gets more attention
or causes more reaction. People sing about it, fight over it, struggle with
it, suffer through it, and die from it. It can raise us up to the highest
level of human endeavor or plummet us to the depths of animal rage. It
can motivate us to fight a war or soften our hearts to perform sublime
acts of kindness.

At one time or another almost all of us find ourselves in love. It is such
a commanding emotion that when we fall in love we often feel out of
control, open, and vulnerable. We are not in charge, the emotion is. We
are left secondarily important to the object of our affection. Love comes
from our heart, but it is so alluring and tempting we believe it comes
from outside ourselves from that special person. Our self-deprecation
will not allow us to own our love; we put it outside ourselves. The beloved
becomes exceptional because we color him or her with our love.

When the object of our love is removed we feel lost and isolated. We
may have an overwhelming sense of loneliness. Our separation becomes

heightened because love allows us momentarily to break through our isolation and know what being together really means. We are left with the grief of our aloneness, which seems all the more powerful because of what we have left behind. It is as if we had a taste of something beyond ourselves, something much more enticing than our selfishness. That taste stirs our interest, and we want more.

Soon we are off pursuing another object of desire. Instead of dwelling in the state of love itself, we search for another person on whom to focus that emotion. We miss seeing the forest because we are focused on a single tree. Again we attempt to hold on to this person as the reason that we love. But circumstances change, the spell is broken, and again we are left grieving. So the whole thing begins anew. In each new instance we recondition ourselves to think of love only in terms of objects.

My own early encounters with love involved enormous swings of energy and emotion. They left me vacillating between extreme highs and lows. I remember well the worry, the awkwardness, and the agonizing self-doubt. For the first time in my memory, the center of my world shifted toward someone else. There was enormous joy in the widening of my concern to include another. I still vividly recall my world imploding when the girl left me. I felt cut off from a treasure that could never be rediscovered. The grief was devastating . . . until someone else caught my eye.

The irony is that many of us go through this process countless times without realizing that love can be universally applied. It does not need to be so narrowly focused. We do not have to single out a particular country, ideal, religion, or person to receive our affection exclusively. When we liberate love from specific objects, and allow it to float freely without restraint, we empower ourselves to move wherever it leads us. This more mature love begins to blanket all of life without distinction. Everything resonates and touches our heart. Action then comes from the source of kindness itself rather than from our willful attempt to be kind.

The tone of universal love is different than romantic love; the feeling is more stable and consistent. It is a perception and an understanding more than an emotional overtone. It does not depend on the presence or absence of anyone or anything. Universal love is free from the emotional reactivity that leads us to harm others. It is not biased, prejudiced, or judgmental. We all have access to this encompassing love because it is inherent in our aliveness. This love is impossible to lose but easily forgotten.

There are so many stories of hospice patients softening their hearts as they relax into their dying. They move from individual love to basic human warmth for all. It is as if the fight is over and now they have time to love. One patient mentioned that her life was so fleeting that all she really had time to do was to offer a little love. Now that she was dying she was less engaged in activity and had time to spread her love around. Maybe this is the secret of loving: we need the time to notice.

Each of us has this ability to love life in its totality, but we limit our hearts by moving too quickly through what we love. Many of us do not take time to make the connections that would bring us into our love. Opening the heart to another's pain, feeling the touch of a breeze on our cheek, experiencing the rapture of a sunrise, catching the fragrant smell of a gardenia, all move our heart into the love that is always accessible. It is ironic that some of us cannot live our love until we are dying.

FINDING OUR AFFECTION

Judy, a twenty-seven-year-old friend, lived with leukemia for a number of years before she decided to have a bone marrow transplant. I met her as she entered the hospital to undergo the procedure. Judy had researched the transplant procedure thoroughly and had prepared for this process as well as anyone could. First her body was completely irradiated. She was then given high doses of chemotherapy for the express purpose of eliminating her own bone marrow. She lost her hair and had considerable nausea and vomiting. After the donor's bone marrow was injected into her, Judy was placed on steroids to offset some of the adverse reactions that accompany the transplant. The steroids caused her body to look bloated and lose its shape. If the bone marrow successfully implants itself into the patient, there is expected to be a graft-host reaction caused by the patient's body rejecting the invasion of the donor's marrow into its own system. This reaction itself can kill the patient. If it does not end the patient's life, the person may have to live with a potentially crippling immune reaction for the rest of his or her life as the body continues to fight off the graft. Depending on one's age, illness, relationship to donor, and so on, the chances of someone surviving this process and living for five years is about 50 percent.

Afterward, Judy said she could never have prepared herself for what she went through, no matter how much she had studied or spoken to other bone marrow recipients. Her body did not graft the bone marrow the first time, and she decided to put herself through this procedure a second time. Each transplant costs hundreds of thousands of dollars. Judy was forced to remain in the hospital almost sixty days and live in the vicinity for another forty days before she could return home.

When Judy made her decision to seek an aggressive cure, she had her whole life ahead of her. She was young, vital, and energetic. Her potential and hope were infinite. Judy said all she cared about was living. She saw it as a contest between medical science and the ravaging disease. She was involved in a struggle to continue to exist. It was a decision to pursue life regardless of the consequences of the treatment. Depending on our age most of us would probably have made the same decision.

These are the extremes we have agreed to endure in order to keep ourselves alive. Our need to live and to have people live is extraordinary. It becomes life at any cost. The goal becomes all-consuming, and our life has little meaning outside the attainment of a cure. Our attention can become so truncated and one pointed that we lose perspective. Our emotions begin to roller coaster with the latest lab results. We can be so consumed with our condition that other people perceive us as unapproachable. This strategy of life at any cost can give us just that, life at the expense of our love. Like the Tin Man in *The Wizard of Oz*, we will eventually have to go in search of our missing heart.

Each one of us can insert our own predicament into this scenario. We do not have to be seeking a treatment for cancer in order to miss our heart's connection. We can be determined to finish a project at work, intent on reading our book, focused on cleaning the house, or absorbed in a conversation. It is all the same fix. Our hearts can become secondary to the focus and completion of the project. People in our lives are then seen as obstacles or aids to the purpose we are pursuing. Relationship becomes a mechanism for fulfilling our own desires and is used as forms of manipulation.

Then suddenly the fight is over. The cancer has advanced beyond its treatable limits, and there is no reasonable place to turn. It begins to dawn on us that what is now at hand is all we will ever have. We can no longer stretch this moment beyond itself and live in an abstract future. Our attention is increasingly drawn toward our immediate aliveness. Since tomorrow is no longer a certainty, we begin to trust where we are now more than where we are going or where we have been. We fall into our aliveness because all the bridges away from this moment have been burned.

This moment is, of course, the only place where life does occur. We sometimes fail to acknowledge this truth because our minds pull us into the dreamlike reality of the past and future. Once we are aligned in time and place, our hearts begin to stir. We have time to be sensitive. We are able to look, take stock of ourselves and our relationships, and appreciate our life in a way that our prior busyness would not permit.

Usually when someone comes into hospice there is an acknowledgment by the doctor, patient, and family that aggressive treatment no longer promises a cure. The patient's world can seem shattered and in disarray. From this depth of despair a few patients begin to orient themselves to their hearts and become transformed in their dying.

Gregory was a fifty-nine-year-old artist and hospice patient with pancreatic cancer. He was living with his partner of twenty-seven years. There was a deep cynicism and anger in Gregory that alienated most people involved in his care. Having been a good cook, Gregory was especially critical of the food he was served. Neither the hospice nor anyone in the house could do anything right. Everything was to be done his way, down to the smallest detail.

Because of the pressure of the spinal tumors, Gregory was forced to spend the last few months of his life in bed. Something changed in him when his activities became limited and he was confined to his bed. Almost overnight he became genuinely warm and approachable.

According to his partner, he was happy for the first time in his adult life. The hospice saw his transformation as resembling that of Scrooge in *A Christmas Carol*. The bewildered hospice nurse asked him if he could explain his sudden change. "Life is wonderful," was all he could say.

Though he could never articulate his conversion, Gregory soon became everyone's favorite patient. He even started to appreciate different styles of cooking. His partner believed the warmth that Gregory showed in his last months of life developed because he was forced to slow down and notice people around him. She said, "Going to bed evened him out. It was the best thing that ever happened to him."

A student once asked a Zen master to tell him the best way to die. The Zen master said simply, "Die quietly." In this uncomplicated statement resides the entire blueprint for a peaceful and affectionate death. As Gregory discovered, affection and warmth are available when there is quietude and simplicity. Our mental turbulence clouds our love. Going to bed allowed Gregory to slow down and open his heart. Like Gregory, if we wish to increase our ability to notice and connect with the world, we need only to become quieter in ourselves. We do not have to go to bed to enter that quietude.

Our life usually becomes simpler as we are dying. Our responsibilities are diminished, and there are fewer demands on us. Potentially we have more time to listen. Dying can force us to settle down, live life a little easier, and allow the heart to flower. A hospice home health aide once remarked that she felt dying was a privilege. When else, she asked, do we really have the time to allow love to express itself? Perhaps moving into love is a privilege reserved for a few quiet people among us.

THE CARING HEART

The speaker for one of our hospice volunteer education programs was a woman who had achieved recognition from the written account of her near-death experience. When she was a young woman she had suddenly lost consciousness and stopped breathing outside a store where she had been shopping. As she felt herself dying she noticed she was no longer in her body. She realized she was outside her physical body but strangely able to hear the thoughts of people in the vicinity. She felt completely calm and tranquil throughout the whole ordeal. Answers to universal questions came to her effortlessly. She said she was completely content to remain dead until she noticed the thoughts of a stranger who was bending over her and attempting desperately to resuscitate her. She said it was not his resuscitation attempts that eventually led her to return. It was his compassion. She could feel his love and concern, and it was that compassion that compelled her to reenter her body.

Compassion arises from our awareness of the suffering of others. It is the spontaneous response of the heart that is accessed when we touch pain in other people. Compassion always approaches people with love. It does not separate them from us nor judge their behavior in any way. We feel people's pain and move psychically into their world to assist in whatever way we can. In order to be with people in their world, we must be willing to experience their pain fully without wavering from it in any way.

We react to pain in another person in exactly the same way we relate to pain in ourselves. If our tendency is to avoid or dismiss disagreeable situations when they arise in ourselves, we cannot be present for someone else who is troubled and needs our help. We usually resist pain because it is unpleasant. But compassion requires more from us than our normal relationship to suffering. It directs us to open our hearts to the pain and journey through the personal hell of another mind without flinching or turning away. When our heart is open to another, it can shine like a beacon and guide the other to his own self-love.

Our hospice chaplain served a dying patient named Tim for over a year. Tim was a machinist at a local plant. Most of that time Tim remained bedridden and unable to function without a great deal of assistance. Each week the chaplain would spend individual time with Tim. He responded well to the company and appreciated the exchanges. Through the aid of the chaplain, Tim would dictate intimate letters to his wife and daughter that he wanted them to read after his death. The weekly process of the chaplain recording Tim's thoughts, editing them, and then having the patient sign the letters, brought the chaplain deeply into Tim's personal world. It was a world of pain and isolation. They shared that pain together.

One day after a new letter had been written Tim remarked that his illness had taught him a great deal about love. When the chaplain asked him to explain what he meant, Tim said, "You have shown me that I am lovable. I never knew that before. It is too bad that I am learning this so late in life, but I probably would have never learned it if it had not been for my illness." Tim had suffered for years from feelings of unworthiness, and because he now felt worthy of the love of others, he was able to express his love in return. He died a much happier man than he had lived.

The power of the chaplain's caring brought Tim into his own heart and proved his ability to love himself and others. Our love can become a path for others to follow. Like begets like. When we feel someone else's caring and concern, it moves us to the same place. As we soften, this other person senses our affection and further opens his heart to us. On and on it goes, deeper into an intimacy that merges both hearts into one. But this intimacy can be threatening because of its very intensity. Sometimes one of the two people involved becomes frightened by the level of involvement and pulls back, retreating into a seemingly safer, but isolated, world.

I worked with Gladys as a social worker for our hospice program. She was an elderly woman who moved into her daughter's home when she became ill. The first time I met Gladys I stayed at her bedside a long time. She desperately needed someone to listen to her experiences. Her family spent very little quality time with her. I barely got a chance to introduce myself before she started sharing her personal life. Occasionally I would nod or ask a relevant question, but the conversation was more of a monologue than a dialogue. On and on she talked. I tried to be as attentive as I could. The image of Gladys I came away with after the first visit was of a tightly coiled spring. All Gladys wanted was an ear and a open mind to listen to her.

The next week I called to arrange another visit. Gladys's daughter answered the phone. She put the phone down to ask her mother when she wanted me to come. I could hear them discussing my visit for several minutes. Finally the daughter returned and hesitantly said that Gladys did not want me to come back. When I asked why, she said her mother felt I talked too much.

At first her comment upset me, and I wondered if I had said something wrong. Upon reflection I knew our conversation had been intimate and lengthy. While we were conversing, we had both been aware of the mutual affection that we shared. This warmth, and her need to connect with someone about her unfinished business, allowed us to approach vulnerable subjects quickly. The exposure had opened her to her own heart. After the visit she must have reflected on the conversation and felt she had unveiled too much of herself. Gladys had become afraid of speaking without her usual protection and had withdrawn into her safe world. I was never again allowed to see her.

The caring heart has its own force and strength. It brings things together without pretension or defensiveness. Through the affection of another we gain the courage to look at ourselves. Usually we underestimate the power of the heart to heal. Coming with our own ideas of how healing occurs, we focus on creating the right physical environment and may miss the subtle effects of a simple interaction, a friendly greeting, or a warm hug. We seem to be healed as much by the intangibles as from a germ-free environment.

If there is too much worry about the competency we bring to a situation, we can easily miss the impact of our hearts. Our caring can become secondary to the rules of our work: being objective in our therapy, completing our progress note, offering the pill on time. Each new responsibility and role can back us away from a genuine human contact. We may end up meeting the person through the veils of our job and miss the healing power of our warmth.

Two nurse friends of mine are very different in temperament and style. Nancy is precise and exact. She is known for her organization and promptness. She does her job thoroughly but without a great deal of warmth and caring. Evelyn is just the opposite. Her documentation is usually late and incomplete, and she is rarely punctual. But she has a wonderful heart. Evelyn mentioned to me how much she admired

Nancy as a nurse. She said she secretly wished she could be like her. I looked at her in shock. I could not believe she was dismissing her extraordinary heart for mere job performance.

The value of the heart's involvement in the healing process is difficult to validate. As professionals, we want to justify the forms and methods we use as the reasons we are effective. Our ego can take a stand on our competency, but it cannot affirm its position with our heart. We look for opportunities to apply our skills only to learn that it is our love that makes an impact and effects change. It leaves us feeling like we really do not do much at all. In fact we do not do much because love is effortless. It does not require our sophistication or philosophies, only our humanity and vulnerability.

A dear friend and hospice mentor of mine tells the story of Roy, a fifty-year-old male hospice patient. He was a man of considerable dignity and stature. Roy was tall and handsome, and much of his sense of self-worth came from his body image. As his illness progressed and his body deteriorated, Roy had considerable difficulty coping with the loss of his value system. The social worker investigated with Roy to see if he could discover a part of himself that remained untouched even as his body withered away. She asked if Roy could get in touch with something in him that was impervious to change, where his dignity remained untouched. They explored this question in great depth.

While this investigation was going on, Roy was being very difficult with his family, ordering and instructing them in multiple ways. The social worker asked Roy if this was the way he wanted to be remembered by his wife and children. Were these the memories Roy wanted to leave behind?

Roy also had a great deal of anxiety and fear over his death. The social worker offered several sessions of guided imagery and relaxation techniques. Roy was working hard to change his manner and reactions. The family was also responding well to several counseling sessions by the social worker. The social worker felt good about her contribution and the techniques she was able to offer. She said she used every technique she knew on this case.

One day as Roy was getting closer to death the social worker asked him what had been the most helpful of all the approaches she had offered. Roy looked at her and said, "What has been most helpful is that I know you care. I know you see many patients, but you make me feel special. You give me the strength to give to my family."

At first the social worker had wanted Roy to validate one of the techniques she had been using—the guided imagery or the relaxation technique. Later she admitted that Roy confirmed what she had always known but could never verify, that it was the power of the relationship that heals. She said there is no substitute for caring. Any or all of our techniques will work when there is a heart behind them. We can develop all the mannerisms and postures of a healer, but unless the person we are facing is held within our affection, little good will be done.

LOVE AND THE EGO

All the activities we learn within the helping professions are solely intended to aid the healing process. When money becomes tight, budgets are trimmed, productivity is highlighted, and functions are economized. The worker is left with less time for patient relationships, less time for caring. The "niceties" are eliminated because they cannot be quantified. We can count the pills we distribute but cannot measure the effect of our love on the patient. The love is cut back and the pills remain, but both are needed.

We tend to consider significant only the things we can see. The activities we do, the thoughts we think, the tasks we complete are a function of our will and our control. We consciously go about performing these jobs with intent and purpose. We can clearly see them. What is unseen, like our love, has a deeper, more fundamental source. It does not come from our ego. It is neither purposeful nor intentional. Universal love cannot be directed by the will. When we act from our ego we are usually being intentional with our love, and this smothers it.

We believe more in our egos than in our love. Love takes a backseat to the functions we perform. This is ironic because love is the real force behind all of our successful caring activities but is seldom given the credit. The ego keeps looking for love but finds only the object of its love. It grasps the music, the poem, the person, and the idea. In seizing the expressions that love takes, it refuses to accept that love is essentially formless. The real power of love is that it does not reside in any specific location. It cannot be held, grasped, possessed, or discovered. It is, therefore, equally available to all.

Our egos would like to do something with the love. We would like to put it to our use. We are less interested in love for its own sake and more interested in the songs, poetry, paintings, and monuments that can be authored in its name. The more we can produce in the name of love, the more love can be substantiated. The more visual we make it, the more we are able to own it and bring it within our sphere of influence. Our egos can then rest on these creations as enduring testimonials to our ability to love.

Owning love, however, is like trying to take possession of the air. Love is infinite and cannot be contained. It is equally available to each one of us. Some people may seem to have more of it than others, but that is only because they do not obscure their love by funneling it into a specific object or person. When we meet such people, their freed hearts release ours in return, and we feel good in their presence. But we should always remember that we are only opening to what is already present within us. These teachers are mirrors, showing us ourselves.

Maureen, an eighty-year-old woman dying of lung cancer, was admitted to hospice care in her daughter's home. She was self-reliant and refused all treatment options before entering hospice. She was determined to die in her own way. Maureen had a long history of going dancing every Saturday night with her husband before he died several years earlier. On the Saturday before she died, Maureen, who was now semiconscious, pleaded, "Can't I go dancing one more time?" Her daughter responded, "Yes, of course you can go." Maureen began to wave her arms in the air as if dancing and replied, "Oh, my feet are so tired." Her daughter, noticing her mother's fatigue, said, "It's okay to sit out a few dances, Mom." Maureen relaxed and fell unconscious.

Later, after Maureen's death, as her children were discussing her life, one of them remarked that she wanted to be placed in an inpatient setting rather than dying at home. After hearing this, one of Maureen's granddaughters asked, "But who would be there to give you permission to dance?"

We are all looking for a way to dance. Dancing represents a free unencumbered spirit whose heart is moving effortlessly through life. We are on this earth for such a short period of time, why try to own and possess it? Life has little to offer of lasting value. Its nature is change and transformation. Why not learn to dance?

As the buds of spring begin their bloom, the fall winds are just over the mountains. We touch a flower, and it has already wilted in our grasp. With all the passing expressions of life moving into new variations, love alone is the one constant. We are here for such a short period of time before we move on. Perhaps all we really have time to do is love . . . and dance.

The night before my friend Liam died, he managed to make his way downstairs to his wife and child. There in his living room he danced with his wife and hugged his child. The next morning as he lay semiconscious with his family by his side, he struggled with the last vestige of his strength to turn and face the window. As he turned, his face became bathed in light. He died five minutes later, moving into his heart.

Love, Compassion, and Intimacy

Reflect on a time when you fell in love. What was that like? How did you act? What did you feel? Did you associate that feeling with an individual person or a unique set of circumstances? What happened to that love over time? Did that love come from the other person or from yourself? How do you know? Was there ever a time when you felt love independently of any special conditions? How was that feeling similar or different from the love for a special individual?

Take something that stirs your heart, something that moves you deeply. It could be a fine piece of music, a beautiful work of art, a good book, a lovely place in nature. Begin to move your love from the specific to the general. For example, if you are particularly fond of a piano concerto by Beethoven, you could begin to spread the love for that particular piece of music to all of Beethoven's music, then to all music. From all music, you could generalize to all sounds, then to all things that create sound, finally blanketing all of creation with your affection. You may have to practice this process many times before it feels genuine. With sincerity the heart can learn to develop a universal warmth for all of life. Notice what happens to this love when your attention becomes diverted to other areas of responsibility. It appears to vanish. In the beginning this affection seems very fragile, but with practice it will arise naturally and spontaneously.

Reflect on the quality of compassion in your life. Think of a time when you were present for someone else's pain. What did that feel like? Was it pleasant or unpleasant? How did you respond? How much difficulty was there in seeing the other person in pain? Upon reflection could you have been more skillful in your response? What must you do to be present with someone's pain without flinching or reacting to the situation? When you are preoccupied with your own problems, are you able to listen to another? What could you do to improve your ability to feel compassion?

Become involved with something that stirs your compassion. Perhaps you could volunteer for a homeless shelter, befriend a person with a terminal illness, or allow yourself to be available to someone who is emotionally troubled or grieving. Compassion takes commitment and time. After you have found the right involvement, take the time to feel the pain of the person or persons you are serving. Attempt to move with empathy into their world by understanding the impact of their immediate situation. Be watchful of two reactions: trying to find a solution to their predicament and moving away from the pain you feel. What happens to the quality of the contact when you are not busy solving the other person's problems? Is this feeling of love specific for this individual, or can you see it as a heartfelt response for the suffering of all beings?

Reflect on your relationship to intimacy. Does intimacy frighten you? If so, what are you afraid will happen if you open to another? Are you afraid of being out of control or losing your boundaries? Reflect on how your relationship with intimacy has affected you throughout your life. Is there a connection between your desire or aversion for intimacy and your ability to love?

Take a walk outdoors alone. Let go of everything that causes you stress. As you walk in silence, let go of all your responsibilities and just be with yourself. Listen to the sounds of nature. Do they move your heart, or do your thoughts keep taking you away to other parts of your life? Is there a conflict between your thoughts and your intention to be quiet? Test this out in other parts of your life.

11 | The Dying Mind

*On the journey of life and death, you must walk
alone; on this journey there can be no taking of
comfort in knowledge, in experience, in memories.
The mind must be purged of all the things it has
gathered in its urge to be secure; its gods and virtues
must be given back to the society that bred them.
There must be complete uncontaminated aloneness.*

—J. KRISHNAMURTI

LEARNING ABOUT PAIN AND SUFFERING in ourselves and
others softens our hearts. We see that pain is universal and that life is
fundamentally beyond our control. Most of us believe we forge our lives
through our own efforts, but pain and death reveal that another power
guides the journey. We have little or no influence on how or when we
will die. We are powerless when we confront the major physical event of
our life. When the dying are able to relinquish their need to control the
outcome and allow the process to unfold naturally, they are often able to
live their last moments peacefully. This lesson of death has implications
for our whole life provided we are willing to learn.

A renowned Buddhist teacher and meditation master named Ajahn
Chah was approached by one of his students when Ajahn Chah was in
declining physical and mental health. He had just gone through a series
of operations and had a brain shunt implanted. The student said that
he thought Ajahn Chah was now living out the teachings that he had
always stressed: his body was deteriorating, his health was precarious,
and there was a possibility of death. Ajahn Chah looked at the student
and said, "Do not speak of these changes so lightly. It is much harder
to go through this than you think." He was saying that it is one thing

to talk about the inevitability of old age, sickness, and death, and yet another to live the experience itself.

We never fully understand what it is like to die until it happens. We may think we know, but the truth is usually vastly different than our expectations. We will almost certainly not be in control of the circumstances. Will there be fear, confusion, lethargy, and fatigue? The process has its own life and may be more difficult than we would like to believe.

Lama Yeshe was a highly regarded Tibetan meditation teacher who was hospitalized after suffering a severe heart attack. Sometime later he wrote a letter to another Tibetan lama about this period of illness. It read: "Never have I known the experiences and sufferings that attended my stay in intensive care. Due to the powerful medication, unending injections, and oxygen tubes just to breathe, my mind was overcome with pain and confusion. I realized it is extremely difficult to maintain awareness without becoming confused during the stages of death. At its worst, forty-one days after I became ill, the condition of my body was such that I became the lord of the cemetery, my mind was like that of an anti-God and my speech like the barking of an old mad dog. As my ability to recite prayers and meditations degenerated for many days, I considered what to do. I did stabilizing meditation with strong mindfulness through great effort, and this was of much benefit. Gradually again I have developed immeasurable joy and happiness in my mind. The strength of my mind has increased, and my problems have lessened and ceased."

Here are two men who spent their lives nurturing their spiritual development, each rising to the challenge of illness and death. Like them, most of us can assume that dying will challenge our capacity to be open and learn, to love, to be gentle and tolerant with ourselves. As D. H. Lawrence once wrote, "Be careful then, and be gentle about death. For it is hard to die, it is difficult to go through the door, even when it opens." At times we will probably be pushed to the limits of our endurance. Our circumstances may well lead us into the darker areas of our psyche where we are surrounded by despair and anger. It will take enormous courage to stay open.

There is no way to foresee the circumstances of our death, or the mental and physical difficulties we will face. We are not able to arrange our dying as we have so many other situations in our life. But trying to control and manipulate the perfect circumstances for our death is not the point. The point is to dive fully into our humanity and die with whatever conditions arise. We work with whatever is actually occurring. We learn from the roller coaster of our dying as we would from a jilted heart or a broken marriage.

Ajahn Chah and Lama Yeshe dedicated their lives to self-knowledge. That dying challenged them is less important than whether they learned and grew from their difficulties. Learning is a much more profound indication of spiritual adeptness than the presence of adversity. Lama Yeshe's letter speaks eloquently for itself. Ajahn Chah's response to his student was an attempt to place the student's theoretical knowledge within the larger context of real wisdom. My guess is these two men were still learning, growing, and teaching even in the presence of intense physical discomfort.

What are the states of mind that usually follow us into severe illness? If we can explore the most common ones while we are still healthy, we may be more prepared when they do occur in ill health. Understanding how we continually fall into these states of mind in health as well as illness will permit us to become more balanced with their energy and more prepared to see them for what they are.

DENIAL

Preparation for dying begins long before we become terminally ill. The actual work happens in every moment of life. We can choose to approach each moment from an attitude of openness and allowance or from fear and resistance. Once we open to the fact of our dying we can begin to accommodate it psychologically. Denial is a refusal to consider the truth. In its darker disguises it is the subconscious counterpart to prejudice and intolerance. Anytime we hold on to our opinions or beliefs and resist new information, we are using denial as a defense.

New information is always accessible. Life continually offers to educate us, but we often refuse to listen. Most of the time we filter the information, preferring to stay with what we have already learned. We feel secure within our opinions. It seems safer to act from our conclusions than to expose ourselves to new information. This is one form denial can take, a disallowing of the possibilities of new growth and discovery, a death of the spirit.

Denial can also serve a healthy function by keeping overwhelming information at bay. It allows the mind to prepare for a difficult message, giving it time to digest and work on the problem. But there is a point when denial will turn on us. If denial persists, at some point it no longer serves as a filtering process and becomes an obstruction to change and accommodation. All too frequently we keep the door shut on the issue far too long. When the issue remains unattended, denial slowly evolves into a rejection of reality. Denial, which was once a healthy defense mechanism, then becomes dysfunctional in its effects.

Pretending that a certain reality does not exist eliminates neither the reality nor its effects on us. Our mental harmony, we already noted, is directly related to the amount of truth we allow to touch us. Since dysfunctional denial closes the truth out completely, it is a very painful state of mind. Shutting down and refusing to believe the obvious takes an enormous amount of mental energy. It does not change the outcome, only our participation in the process. When we deny, we live in an imaginative world that is waiting to fall apart. Dysfunctional denial on occasion must be addressed directly for everyone's benefit.

I worked with Rita, a young mother dying of breast cancer. She was married with two young children aged twelve and fourteen. The hospice became involved with the case when the woman had only a few weeks to live. Rita slept most of the time but would occasionally attempt to get out of bed and continue her roles as mother and wife. The family was ignoring Rita's weakened condition and was encouraging Rita to be active. The attending physician had become frustrated after repeated attempts to communicate Rita's end-of-life condition to the family. No one in the family, not even the patient, was willing to face the consequences of the illness. The family situation tore at the hearts of the hospice staff. There was such sadness in the two young children and the endearing husband as they pretended that Rita would not die. The situation turned from bad to worse as Rita began to fall regularly as she routinely forced herself out of bed. The family refused to help her in any way.

The family's dysfunctional denial was creating an enormous amount of suffering for everyone and bordered on physical neglect of the patient. As the social worker on the case, I called a family meeting and discussed the condition of the patient in stark terms. I understood they wanted their mother to get better but that was not going to happen. They argued that a miracle could always occur. I took their hope away and would not let it return. There was an overwhelming outpouring of grief and tears. Slowly the family regrouped and started to plan for Rita's care. After the meeting the family rallied around Rita, said their goodbyes, and cared for her until she died. The father was able to take the lead and assume many of Rita's roles.

It is almost always better to leave denial alone and not force the issue. A patient's physical deterioration usually provides sufficient feedback for the patient to break through denial without anyone interfering. Everyone has his own timing. To intrude on denial prematurely can often upset the mental balance needed for a sane resolution of a crisis. The clinician travels a fine line in forcing the issue of denial, because when a defense of this strength is removed, it is never certain what behaviors may erupt in its absence. In rare cases, however, denial can be so counterproductive that it disrupts the care and well-being of everyone involved. In Rita's case, the denial was so dysfunctional that it was more devastating to ignore the situation than to address it openly. There was little choice but to act.

At times we all pretend to be what we are not. Denial is no different. It is simply the reluctance to break a bond of love—a love of life, of family, and of influence. When we can connect with the pain behind the denial, it allows our heart to open to the patient. I have often heard hospice workers say they are frustrated with the denial of a patient or family: "The death would be so much better if he would talk about it with his wife." That is our denial of where the patients are in their process. Ultimately, to rush anyone through his or her growth usually results in more tragedy than help.

THE LOSS OF CONTROL

Television has exaggerated the dying process. We may have watched dramatic scenes in which actors writhe in physical pain yet remain emotionally stoic, directing the family through their last moment. Usually these representations are not true to life. Enormous advances in the delivery of medications almost always assures the dying patient relief from physical suffering. It is also difficult for a patient who faces the total ending of all that she has known to remain emotionally distant and aloof to her death. Dying has a way of bringing the person back in touch with her emotional life. For patients with a terminal prognosis, the time of death usually finds the person in a coma and unable to communicate. As with Lama Yeshe, the patient may have difficulty establishing clarity and focus as his mental and physical energy waxes and wanes. All of these changes force the patient to deal with the loss of physical and mental control.

Many dying patients witness a steady loss of influence. Their roles in life begin to diminish as the illness erodes their vitality. As these changes occur, patients may experience both grief and a sense of worthlessness. These emotional reactions indicate that their self-worth has been tied to their activities, to the things they do. When they can no longer do as much, they feel useless. Having cultivated their sense of self only through their roles and responsibilities, they have nothing to fall back on to achieve personal fulfillment.

The dying often use their activities to stay in control. They may go through a period of time in which they are very engaging and interactive. These activities can serve two purposes. They allow the patient to feel worthwhile and productive, and they blunt the emotional intensity of dying. Engaging in activities can sometimes be a subtle form of denial.

Cindy was a hospice patient who was very vocal about the benefits of the hospice program and equally expressive in her distaste for physicians who were afraid to communicate honestly with their patients. She had been through a horror story with her personal physician and eventually was forced to switch doctors because of his persistent evasiveness concerning her prognosis. Thereafter she became an excellent proponent of hospice care. Much to her delight, Cindy's eloquence was discovered by a local medical school, and she began to speak in front of medical students about the need for honest communication between doctor and patient. Cindy also agreed to perform several public service announcements for the hospice program about how to face one's death and dying. Clearly Cindy was appreciating the attention and was performing a service for both herself and others.

Several weeks later Cindy began to succumb to her own progression of illness and became too weak for any additional speaking engagements. Suddenly she became terrified of the very dying process about which she had been speaking eloquently two weeks earlier. Cindy found the idea of dying very different than the fact. So long as she was relatively healthy, she was in complete control of herself, her audience, and her subject matter. All of that changed when she began to weaken. Acting had been one way she had remained in control of her life. With the loss of her ability to perform, there was nothing left to blunt the effects of her dying.

André Malraux once wrote, "There is no death....There is only me...me...who is going to die." A person at the end of his life sees himself dying before his own eyes. Death is no longer an abstraction. It is felt in the bones. One indication is a diminishing self-image, which is often tied to power and prestige. It is painful for the dying patient to watch the diminution of his self-worth. This erosion can lead to mood swings and irritability. He may begin to strike out in disagreeable ways in an attempt to reassert his lost influence. Suddenly he becomes more demanding, calling for help at all hours. He may become more critical and less tolerant. Nothing seems to satisfy him completely.

Harold was a kindly man appreciated and loved by his family and friends. When he became ill with cancer he saw his life change considerably. As he reflected on the changes, he would shake his head and say that he was not the man he used to be. He noticed his children offering him the emotional and physical support that he once offered them. He said he felt as if the parental roles had been switched. His relationship with his wife also changed. With the chemotherapy and physical weakness their sexual relationship ended. His wife started shouldering many of the responsibilities that he had always assumed.

When Harold became bedridden he grew increasingly annoyed and frustrated. He found himself irritable and critical. Neither Harold nor his family could understand these changes in his temperament. The family was afraid to address them for fear of upsetting Harold. Since he was dying they avoided any confrontation with him at all. This upset Harold even more. He felt disengaged and patronized.

Harold's family asked the hospice social worker to become involved. The social worker pointed out the connection between Harold's annoyance and his loss of control. Based on the social worker's intervention, the family stopped tiptoeing around Harold's illness and began calling him on his mood swings and irritable disposition. They also started to include him in family decisions and once again turned to him for advice and comfort. Harold's irritability lessened, but his dying remained a difficult adjustment. Harold was never able to adjust to the role of being a patient, nor could he see himself as having value outside of his activities.

Many of us feel we lose our purpose for living when our roles and activities decrease. If we have been successful in business and are suddenly forced to retire, our identity remains fixed as a businessperson even in retirement. We have no other image to fall back on as we become less engaged. The retired elderly are not held in high esteem like the young; wisdom and character are not valued as much as youth and energy. We do not sufficiently honor our character development nor give adequate time to our inward growth to feel comfortable living without producing. We believe our sense of worth is predicated on our functionality, on being active and useful. As a culture we appreciate ambition and drive because of where they will take us, not because they are traits of a decent human being. If our character is appreciated at all, it is usually seen for what it will bring us, what fortunes it will reap. Intelligence is valued because it smooths the way for our education, congeniality because it helps us climb the ladder of success.

The low value that we as a society place on spiritual growth may explain why we have so much unworthiness in this country. We spend very little time looking inward and appreciating who we are. Our attention is usually focused outward on the things we have done. These accomplishments, not the inward qualities of integrity and kindness, qualify us as being worthy and honorable.

Given our emphasis on ambition, it is easy to see why we suffer when we die. Our ambition does not help us through death. Rather, it leads to a hardness of character that precludes learning, flexibility, and openness of mind, qualities that are the hallmark of an expansive death. When we have spent our life cultivating ambition, our character moves with that trait in death. It leads us to believe that there is something to do or accomplish during our dying. This emphasis on doing can separate us from the intimacy of the moment and lead us away from our hearts. It is within our hearts that fulfillment lies and where death can be explored.

Being in control suggests an attitude of individualism and self-sufficiency. It assumes an influence that is not typically borne out by experience. A need to control distances ourselves from others, and we experience a sterile aloneness, missing the connection and mutual support offered by relationships. In addition, we obstruct our connection with the spiritual.

Dying offers a rare opportunity to compare what the culture has told us about ourselves and what death shows us we are. Losing control does not diminish us as human beings. Our consciousness is still whole regardless of whether we lose an arm, a leg, or are confined to bed. We are not less of a person because we can no longer go to work and produce. One of the greatest teachings of death is that the great importance we place on our activities is distorted. Dying dissolves the illusion of self-importance, and yet we are still here with our hearts intact.

LOSING OUR SENSE OF SELF

Studies of people with chemically induced changes in consciousness reveal similar experiences to the slow loss of identity that dying patients recount. Not only do people report understanding that they are more than the summation of their roles, but some also report a sense of existence beyond their mind and body experience. Some speak of feelings of lightness and joy as they understand they are still whole and complete even in the absence of their bodies, minds, and self-images.

Similar stories are reported by long-term meditators. In the Buddhist tradition there are many individuals who have arrived at a profound understanding of the nature of self and other. They speak of the certainty of knowing what they are not; they are not their roles, not their body, and not their experiences. The consistent understanding achieved through all these reports leads us to believe in its validity. Maybe there is something more fundamental to our humanity than this body and brain that thinks, talks, and acts. If there is, then death can potentially guide us to that essential nature by eliminating everything else along the way. It can be a tool for showing us how we continuously misrepresent ourselves.

After everything has been taken away we still have our aliveness. There is no gradation to aliveness. There are no indications of it tapering off with our dying, for it does not seem to depend upon the mind or body at all. Our aliveness is the ground floor of our being on which we build our responsibilities and give ourselves an identity. We can return to it after dying takes away everything else. Hospice patients can sometimes connect with their aliveness even in the face of physical trauma. This sense of being awake can be a refuge from their illness.

Charles was a fundamentalist Christian who had lung cancer and was having a difficult time breathing. Every breath was labored and forced. Charles was frightened at losing control of a normally involuntary function like breathing. He would try to reassure himself by saying it was God's will that he was dying, but he remained agitated and restless. We discussed the difficulty of losing control of this basic function of the body. It was indeed God's will that he was dying, I said, but was it not also God's will that he was still alive? I suggested that his breath was an indication of his aliveness. Maybe he could take refuge in the breath of life rather than on his fear of losing that breath. He could then be reassured of God's immediate will rather than what God's will might eventually become. His aliveness, I said, could take him through this entire experience and drop him off at God's door. Charles seemed to quiet a little as he began to rest with his breathing. He died before

I could follow up and visit him again, but he told his wife he felt God was somehow connected to his breath.

When we examine our aliveness we see something more fundamental than the experiences we have. We must first be alive in order to have an experience. Death removes all experience. It eliminates the entire world of the senses, from which all experience is derived. If the near- and after-death stories are true, however, our aliveness continues after death. Death cannot take away our aliveness because our aliveness is more fundamental than death. When we siphon off all experiences from our aliveness, we are left with pure awareness, an essence that is beyond death or defeat.

We are very strongly conditioned to believe in our experiences, so strongly that we often feel we are living at the whim of circumstances. Our experiences seem to change from pleasant to unpleasant and back again. Good times and bad, sickness and health, poverty and wealth are all circumstances that we either avoid or pursue. But awareness is beyond all pursuit and avoidance. While it is more basic to life than any situation we encounter, we need enormous faith to trust in this aware-ness over our experiences. Dying can teach us about trusting.

TRUSTING THE PROCESS

I played a game when I was young where I would fall backward into the arms of another person. I remember the trust that was needed to allow myself to fall and believe the other person would catch me. The other person never failed to do his job, but I was always in fear whenever I played the game. Dying seems to have that sense of free fall. We have no memory of experiencing it before and therefore have little trust in the process. It may feel like jumping out of an airplane without a parachute. But the actual process may be more like the Ojibway saying: "Some-times I go about pitying myself, and all the time I am being carried on great winds across the sky."

Most of us believe we have forged our lives through our own efforts. Death disrupts our normal control over things. It seems to happen beyond our influence, and there is nothing we can do about it. An important teaching of death is the revelation of just who has been guiding our journey all along.

Dying without fear takes a great deal of trust, a trust that can help us live with more faith, if we can understand our need to control. Death teaches us the power of letting be, of noninterference and surrender. The process of dying is completely natural. The laws of nature govern death as they do our lives. It is difficult to understand the power of not doing, of leaving these natural laws alone, when we have always attempted to act our own course. Death can teach us when to leave things alone and when to act.

The dying frequently seem to learn this lesson. There is often a sense of relaxing into the process, especially if the patient is older and has lived a full life. At the time of death, we may be forced to deal with surrender and trust, yet the same laws that govern life and death are working on us right now. Through surrendering we learn to develop greater trust and reliance on that which we cannot see or touch objectively.

Lucia was a hospice patient who was able to connect with this trust. She was a modest woman with a natural honesty and ease with others. Her daughter said she did not flinch when the doctor told her that her cancer was beyond treatment. She simply asked how long she had to live. There was never any self-pity or confusion. Lucia just continued to do what she had always done with the same degree of contentment and calmness. She was particularly interesting to me because she would talk about dying when I introduced the topic. There was no sense of avoidance or need to bring the subject up. I asked Lucia about her quietude in the face of her death. She said life was about trusting in something larger than her own desires. She could not explain it, but she knew everything she went through was for the greater good. "My illness," Lucia said, "confirms that belief. It does not threaten me in any way."

Unlike Lucia, most dying patients look for assurance that they will be okay. But no one who is living can guarantee a safe journey through death. We look to our religions to assure a safe passage, but our religion usually throws us back on our morality. "If you have been good you have nothing to fear." But have we been good enough? Goodness is a relative term. Our moral evaluation of ourselves will not allow us to relax and trust.

Trust has nothing to do with moral courage. It occurs when we have nowhere else to turn, when we reach the end of our need to control. When we are dying we cannot turn around and go back toward health. Dying requires that we take the step without proof. We walk through the door. We cannot turn around and go back, so we walk through. The end. No guarantees, no certainty, no assurance. We walk, taking each step not from fear but from love, because a great mystery is blessing each footfall. Our hearts understand that mystery and feel the joy. It is the mystery returning to itself.

Letting Go of Control

What are the advantages of denying the truth rather than accepting things the way they are? Think of a time when denial protected you from a truth that was too devastating to accept. How did denial help you through that time? When were you actually able to recognize the truth? What had changed in the meantime? Reflect upon the pain you felt when you first understood what had happened. Now think about the tension you carried while you were pretending it was not true.

The next time you find yourself refusing to accept something, take a moment to notice your reactions. Use your reactions as a cue to question whether you are denying anything about the situation. Find a quiet place and watch what you are feeling and thinking. What is it that you refuse to accept, and why? Be honest and keep returning to your aversion.

Reflect on your need to control when events are chaotic and unpredictable. What are the feelings that arise, and how do you handle such situations? Reflect on how much time and energy you spend arranging events, hoping they will turn out the way you desire. How does this interfere with being spontaneous and creative? How do other people react when you step in and attempt to control the situation? How do you feel when someone does that to you?

Become aware of what you can and cannot control. There are obvious events such as the weather, the passage of time, and involuntary bodily conditions that are beyond your control. What about your emotions, reactions, and fears? Are you able to control these? Do you decide whether to be angry or happy? Give more attention to the moods, thoughts, and attitudes that influence your life, and ask yourself if these are under your control. Do you create a desire or a fear, or do they occur on their own when certain conditions are present?

Reflect on who you are. Think of all the qualities that define you as a person. Ask yourself if this list captures the essence of who you are. What is missing? If you were dying and began to lose your roles and responsibilities, would you be diminished as a person? Would anything remain?

Ask yourself who you are, and directly observe the answer you give. "I am my body. I am my emotions. I am my thoughts." But if you can observe your body, your moods, your thoughts, how could you also be them? The very act of observation places the object outside of your being. Continue to spend time asking yourself, "Who am I?" and see where the question leads. Let the question sit with you without rushing to answer it. Does the question disturb you or bring greater peace of mind?

The Buddha summed up his teaching by saying, "Cling to naught." You can approach this wisdom through practicing the skillful means of letting go. The practice of letting go is as close as you can come to practicing your death moment after moment. Letting go can be either an act of release or simply a moment of nonattachment. All the exercises and reflections in this book are methods for letting go. Letting go means permitting life to be as it is without resistance. It means allowing the moment to die without further embellishment and thought. It is the ultimate act of trust.

Reflect on what it means to let go, to let be, to trust and leave things as they are. Reflect on how you usually manipulate events rather than simply trusting and letting them be. How easy is it for you to let go of your desires, resentments, angers, or frustrations? What does it feel like to hold on to your pain and pride?

Practice letting go. The next time you find yourself mentally holding on to a past, current, or future event, release it, and let it fall away. Letting go does not have to be developed, it has only to be done. Instead of trying to understand everything or figure things out, simply let go. Let go of your desires, expectations, and fears. Let go of your worries and your remorse. Let go of your life and your death. Let go and release everything to be just as it is. Nothing special to be, no wounds to heal, no past or future to bind you. Let everything be without picking it up as "me" or "mine."

12 | Understanding Grief

*[Grief] is the ashes from which the phoenix rises
and the mettle of rebirth. It returns life from the living
dead. It teaches that there is nothing absolutely true
or untrue. . . . Grief will make a new person out of
you, if it doesn't kill you in the making.*
—STEPHANIE ERICSSON

GRIEF IS AN INTEGRAL PART of all of our lives. Death takes our loved ones, relationships die, businesses fail, jobs are lost, marriages end. Suddenly we are terminally ill and must prepare to lose everything. If we are to survive a loss, we must learn to let go of the very thing we have depended on to sustain our life. Grief is a common denominator of human existence that unites us all.

I was once giving a bereavement talk at a memorial service for the hospice I was working for in Plymouth, Massachusetts. Before the talk I walked outside the church and strolled through the graveyard, looking at the dates on the gravestones. Some were so old the carved date had eroded away. Others, I could see, were from the seventeenth and eighteenth centuries. Walking through the graveyard, I was deeply moved by how long humanity has mourned and suffered from loss. As we saw in the epigraph in chapter 9, the Buddha once remarked to his monks that we have cried more tears for the loss of our loved ones than all the waters contained in the great oceans of the world. When we grieve we join with all the hearts of the past who have loved and lost.

A few years ago I attended a workshop on holotropic breathwork. During the sessions each student is instructed to breathe in short rapid breaths for a long period. This is accompanied by loud vibrating music. The breathing and music together move the listener beyond the normal state of consciousness. I went to an area of my mind where there was grief and began to feel the sadness of the losses I had incurred. Suddenly something changed, and I shifted away from my personal grief into what I can only describe as a black hole of grief. There was nothing else but grief. There was no beginning or end to this blackness, which was filled with the losses of all humanity. It was no longer my grief but the grief from all losses, from all of time. I began to sob uncontrollably. One of the spotters on the retreat was concerned and came over, but I waved her away because I did not want to be disturbed from this view of grief. I was fully engaged in learning about an emotion that had always seemed to be just below my normal consciousness. After that event, grief became much more acceptable and understood.

The Buddha's remark that humankind's tears are greater than the world's oceans elevates grief to the prominence it deserves. Grief is timeless in scope and infinite in breadth. As a child I remember seeing my mother weeping in the kitchen more than a year after my grandmother died. I asked her what was wrong, and she said she was grieving the loss of her mother. I was surprised and said, "But Mother, that happened over a year ago." I will always remember her reply. She looked at me and said gently, "It never ends."

Loss will always be a part of living. In some way the prospect of loss defines our capacity for joy—joys of having and belonging. We cannot know love without also knowing its absence. We want so desperately to feel the intimacy and caring of another person's heart, but we also want to avoid losing that connection once it is found. How could we ever have one without the other? Having and losing complement each other throughout the duration of our lives.

Each of us is asked to hold a portion of life's grief within the heart. For some, the magnitude of their loss is unendurable, the weight too much to bear. Others are less burdened by grief, their lives unencumbered by dramatic loss. Although grief is not evenly apportioned, everyone lives with some. If we can understand and accept grief as part of our humanity, our suffering will diminish.

HOW WE GRIEVE

Grief contains a variety of states and emotions including anger, sadness, rage, despair, depression, numbness, lethargy, and emotional exhaustion. In one moment we can be desperately grieving the loss of our loved one, missing him deeply, and in the next, extremely angry with him for dying. It is not a rational emotion. It does not make logical sense to anyone, including the person grieving. This is one of the problems associated with grief. The bereaved often feel as if they are losing their minds. They usually find themselves easily distracted and unable to focus or attend to the tasks of daily life.

Bereavement is a process of confusion and disorientation. Grief, although illogical, is a sane emotion. The world of the grieving has become disjointed. Their lives as they have known them have been severed forever. Everything they have worked to assemble is dismantled by a single event. The normal reaction to a world in disarray is confusion and bewilderment. Grieving is a sane reaction to chaos.

Grief is one of the most difficult emotions because it is often accompanied by a sense of hopelessness. It is one thing to have an emotion like anger and know from experience it will end; it is another to grieve and know our life has changed forever. From the view of the bereaved there is no conceivable dawn after the darkness of grief. There is nothing beyond hopelessness. Grief can seem like a black hole where no light can penetrate. That blackness is the darkness of not knowing, of not understanding, of having no firm ground on which to stand. When our main life support system is another human being and that human being dies, it leaves us without meaning or purpose. "Why go on?" is the despairing voice of the bereaved.

Recovering from grief requires passing through this perception of meaninglessness and coming out the other side. Grief holds the potential for a great deal of understanding and wisdom. We cannot push grief away for very long. It forces us to deal with it, to acknowledge its unpleasantness and continue on. Usually we avoid unpleasant situations at all costs, but there is nowhere to hide from grief. Like chronic physical pain, the emotion is unremitting and does not allow us to distract ourselves for very long.

Because of its ceaseless quality, grief holds the promise of opening us to the way things are. When pain is so acute, our usual distractions offer no relief. A capacity we rarely use is required—our complete attention. Since there is nothing we can place between ourselves and the emotion, the emotion itself has to be attended to. When the mind is focused with that degree of sincerity it can go very deeply into itself. Like a stone dropped into a well, the mind penetrates to the base of its being. It surrenders its excuses, its defenses, its blame, and looks at the rawness of things as they are. Within the turmoil of grief, it is possible to access immense strength and love.

When our hospice in Massachusetts began to serve Norma's husband, Norma had already lost two of her four children in separate tragedies. One had died of childhood cancer, the second from a freak drowning incident. Now Norma's husband was in the last stages of pancreatic cancer. When I first heard about Norma in the team meeting, I wondered how I would ever approach this woman. She must have recoiled so deeply into herself she would be virtually unreachable. The woman I met on the visit was very different from my expectations. She seemed serene and composed. As we started speaking, I felt as if I were in the presence of someone vastly superior in emotional intelligence. She was totally in her grief. She would speak about her husband and children, grieving fully, but with a sense of self-ease and gentleness. She was full of warmth and caring. Her conversations always seemed to contain nuggets of wisdom. She would say things like, "My pain somehow connects me with people. It makes me feel intimate with everyone." I was eager to explore this understanding with her, but all she could say was, "Pain will take you there."

It was obvious after many such discussions with Norma that she had used grief to bring herself closer to life. There had probably been many moments when she could have understandably sided with self-pity and become cynical and angry. Given her multiple losses almost everyone would have understood these reactions. Instead she lived with her pain and grew through it. Her pain opened her to self-knowledge, and she was able to bring peace to her heart despite her grief.

Grief contains the ambiguity of the relationship with the lost one. It is difficult to grieve because we do not grieve from clarity but rather from the confusion, guilt, anger, hurt, and love that was the relationship. When the person dies we grieve her entire personality, some part of which we were at odds with while she was alive. There is a tendency to idealize the person and not allow both the good and bad behavior into our grief. We feel we betray her if we think about the side of her we did not like. To grieve normally requires the dead to pass through our mind and heart completely, just as they were while alive.

Sometimes we feel we are disloyal to the person who has died if our grief abates and we return again to a more complete lifestyle, as if reengaging fully in life somehow undermined the love we had for the person who died. If our grief lessens, does that mean we no longer honor the relationship we had together? Thoughts like these perpetuate the grief and complicate its resolution. We think our hearts have only so much space, and if we let someone in we must put someone else out. Often guilt and shame surface when the widows or widowers begin to have romantic interests. They feel if they do not dwell in painful memories of the loved one, they are not honoring their lifetime commitment and vow. Their central human focus for so many years is now playing second fiddle to a new person.

For a brief period of time I worked as a social worker at a nursing home in Houston. I was assigned certain floors and would walk the corridors, regularly stopping in rooms along the way to chat with the residents. I passed one such room several times during the first few weeks of my job and noticed an elderly woman caring for a comatose patient. One afternoon I stopped in and began to chat with the woman. She told me she was the mother of the patient. I inquired about her daughter. She said her daughter attempted suicide by hanging when she was thirteen years old. The mother had discovered her daughter before she had died but not in time to save her from her vegetative state. That had occurred thirty years ago.

The mother started to cry as she told me of the guilt and pain she lived with each day. Thirty years ago the relationship with her daughter had been strained, and she blamed herself for the hanging. There had been very few days she had not visited her daughter in all those years. The rest of her life had been placed on hold. She had divorced her husband and cut herself off from many of her friends. After conversing with her for some time, it became obvious that she would not allow herself to stop grieving because to stop would exonerate her from the role she had in the suicide attempt. Her grief was her punishment.

We are often our own worst enemy. We can use the pain of our grief for penance and restitution for an unfulfilled promise or because we do not want to relinquish the special place a person once held in our hearts. This allows our love, which once held infinite potential and hope, to turn against us and create its opposite. We use the person's memory to keep us in place, to confine us in time and space. Limiting ourselves in this way, we become stagnant, and stagnation does not honor the love that lives on in our hearts. The love in our hearts cries out for engagement. It wants to connect and regain intimacy.

In recovering from grief, our first priority is to perpetuate our love rather than limit it to a single memory. The ability to love is what will keep us engaged in a meaningful way. If we confine our love to the deceased and do not reengage, we will find ourselves reflecting on life in the past tense, this moment never being as fulfilling as the time when he or she was alive. Our lives will essentially be over even before death takes us.

Our hearts have infinite space to honor all loves lost and gained. We do not have to be afraid of dishonoring that special person if we love again. That person lives on in our hearts and will never die, and we venerate him or her each time we love. Our love becomes stronger and more powerful because everyone is contained within it, including the deceased. Each time we access our love we are honoring all loved relationships.

WHY WE GRIEVE

Grief is a bittersweet emotion. Even though it hurts we subconsciously long for the grief to continue. Through the hurt we have access to the memories and the connection we crave. We want the connection without the pain, but the two coexist. We have to hurt to connect again with the person we have lost. We are willing to put up with the pain if we can still have the residue of the relationship, the remnants, at least, of a loved one who now exists only in memory.

Memory is not an adequate substitute for the real thing. We entertain it for a while but eventually we turn away because an imaginary relationship is unfulfilling. Our hearts yearn for a full and active life, not an imaginary one. A relationship is supportive only when it is alive and active, when it is vital and full of energy and growth. Memories can never serve this function because memory alone cannot sustain life.

As we heal, we begin to understand that when we dwell on what we used to have, we become as dead as the person we mourn. It is a one-sided engagement with a past time, and it leaves us disconnected from the present moment. Ultimately memory has no active life at all, although it can be skillfully used to recover from loss.

Christ said, "Let the dead bury the dead." He may have meant that only those who are unconcerned with their spiritual growth will dwell on the past, and that our guilt, remorse, and grief keep us dead to the living world. If we are living in the present moment, the influence of the past is minimal. Whenever we bring in the past and superimpose it on this moment, we kill part of our aliveness. We limit our actions and thoughts to what we have already done, and we limit ourselves to what we have already been. We should view our memories as old relics that have limited use as current reference points. Grief is then understood as a process of healing ourselves to the past in order to move our lives into the present.

As time lessens the pain, our grief undergoes a transformation. We grieve the loss of the sensory contact but not the loss of the love, because the love is still here. Our love made the relationship; the body was only love's reference point. Warmth and affection come from the heart's connection and are not dependent on the person's physical presence at all. AVection remains viable whether the person is in the same room, across the country, or dead. As a Shoshone medicine man said, "If the dead be truly dead, why should they still be walking in my heart?"

One of the hospice social workers related the story of Edward, who had lost his wife after fifty-five years of marriage. Edward and Ellie had loved each other dearly and were almost inseparable. They had met when Edward was fifteen years old, so he barely knew what life was like without Ellie. After her death he missed her terribly. He kept all the details of her life just the way they were while she was alive. Ellie's clothes were in her closet untouched, and her bureau was filled with the trinkets of her life. He used the hospice bereavement services for the considerable support he needed during the first year of his mourning.

About a year and a half after Ellie's death, the social worker visited Edward in his home. The house seemed pretty much back to normal. Edward had given Ellie's clothes and possessions away and occasionally was "visiting with a few female friends." The social worker inquired about the change. Edward responded by saying that over time he realized Ellie was still with him in his heart. "It is like an extended vacation. I don't see her, but I still love her. I miss her terribly, but the connection is still there, and she is telling me to go out there and live!"

Edward understood that Ellie was only a heartbeat away. Honoring Ellie did not mean focusing on her memory to the exclusion of all else. Edward celebrated his long life with Ellie by honoring the love he held for her every day. He used their love to open to a new life that included a new relationship. Edward married one of his female friends two years later.

GRIEF AND CHANGE

There is an acute sense of tragedy in our grief because we do not live comfortably with death, with discontinuity, with change. One of the mysteries of the mind is that we can live our years in a world that is defined by change and deny its influence on our lives. Shakespeare in Julius Caesar put it this way: "Of all the wonders that I have heard, it seems to me most strange that men should fear, seeing that death, a necessary end, will come when it will come."

We usually try to make everything last forever. We buy a new car and expect it to stay new, waking in the middle of the night to check if anyone has sideswiped it. When the inevitable dent does occur we grieve the loss of its permanent newness. We try to push life beyond its natural conclusion. We play it as if we could perform infinite encores. We do not allow it to end on time.

In attempting to perpetuate things long past their natural life span, we live at the expense of a greater harmony and contentment. If we include loss in our philosophy of life at all, it is only as tragedy or error, for which we blame anyone or anything. So grief catches us by surprise when it rudely interrupts our ideal world. Our emotional well-being fluctuates with each scratch and dent in life. Our grief is partially a self-righteous resentment of the laws of the universe. Our longing to recover what is lost is an indication of how little we attune to the rhythms of nature.

There is a rhythm to grief as well. It is as natural and normal to grieve as it is to lose. It is said that even the Buddha mourned the loss of his two chief disciples. The mind has its own harmony, its own way of regaining balance and stability after a loss. That process is called grief.

Opening the Heart to Grief

Reflect on the losses in your life. Think about all the losses you endured when you were a child or an adolescent: your pet animal died, your toys broke, you were jilted in a relationship, you lost recognition, love, or hope. Feel the pain associated with those losses. Stop and reflect on each one. What was the effect of those losses on you? Is the sadness you feel associated with one loss or the accumulated losses in your life?

Walk slowly through a graveyard and look at the gravestones. Read the names, the dates, the inscriptions. Think of the grief that so many people suffered at a single individual's death. Feel the grief in your own heart and connect that grief with all the people in that graveyard and all the graveyards of the world. The pain is no longer personal but universal. Is it easier to bear your allotment of grief when you understand the universality of the emotion?

Reflect on your willingness to feel sad or to mourn. How comfortable are you with this emotion? How comfortable are you seeing others grieve? Do you encourage them to get on with their life, or do you allow their grieving the space and time it deserves? Reflect on how you distract yourself from feeling grief. What are your strategies for avoiding pain? Do you seek companionship or entertainment as a way to distract yourself?

Take out photos of someone you were close to who has died. Feel the sadness and grief of the loss. Bring up old events and memories associated with that person. Share them with someone who also loved the person. Feel the pain of the grief. Sit with it silently without any distractions. Feel the bittersweet quality of grief. Do not try to understand or analyze it in any way. Just feel grief for what it is, and let it be.

Reflect on a person you love who is living. Does your love for that person change if there is physical distance between you? Reflect on what is important in this relationship. Would there be any relationship at all without the affection and caring? Does the presence or absence of the person diminish the caring?

Feel the heart's connection with the person you love, the warmth of feeling, the genuine affection. Picture the person in your mind and feel the substance of the relationship. Does this diminish with time or space? The next time your loved one is away, see if your affection is diminished in any way. Now think of someone you love who has died. Again feel the connection of the heart. Is it as real and as genuine now as it was when he or she was alive? What does this tell you about the heart and death? What are you really grieving when you mourn?

13 | The Ending of Time

This life of one day is a life to rejoice in.
Because of this, even though you live for just one
day, if you can be awakened to the truth, that
one day is vastly superior to an eternal life. . . .
If this one day in the lifetime of a hundred years
is lost, will you ever get your hands on it again?
—DOGEN

GRIEF IS NOT THE FINAL LESSON in our growth through death and dying. We go through our grief to something more fundamental, something that is as close to us as our breath, the breath we lose at death. This is the ultimate comfort for hearts that mourn and is available throughout our lives if we allow ourselves to find it. We discover it by deciphering the codes of time. What are these lessons that the dying offer about time, and how do they promise a greater freedom for us all?

The dying have an enormous amount to teach us about the preciousness of time. Most of us have a great deal of confusion around time. We want more and more of it, yet we do not fully live within the time we do have. The future weighs heavily on many of us, and the past burdens us with remorse and guilt. We can find ourselves procrastinating and delaying our living with excuses and denials. We spend so much time rehearsing where we are going or regretting where we have been that only occasionally do we acknowledge the present moment. Time slips by unnoticed until we suddenly awaken and find death at our doorstep.

Working with the dying has awakened me to the fleeting and precarious moment on which I rest. Each morning when I enter the hospice office I pass the list of patient names written on the hospice boards. I know these names represent a cross-section of life that fits my own demographics. I often feel I am walking past my own name. In my clearer moments the psychological distance between the hospice patient and me narrows. I recognize that I could—will—be one of them. Suddenly I too am running out of time. Every day I find I have to allow death to influence the way I think about time, or the urgency quickly fades. All too easily I assume my health will continue and my life will extend endlessly into the future.

We often look to the future with a false sense of realism, as if we were assured that it will actually occur. But when we realize that dying is inevitable, we can no longer project ourselves into a certain future. Each moment becomes alive and vital without anticipating how it might evolve. We can no longer pretend that life is anything other than what it has always been—an immediate process.

Understanding the immediacy of death rearranges our priorities. It takes away our strategies of avoidance. If it is happening now, I take responsibility for it. I do not delay my response. One experienced hospice nurse tells me she can no longer go to bed angry at her husband. "There isn't time," she says, "to hold resentment." No more delay or postponement. We now hold ourselves accountable and responsible. We face ourselves in honesty.

When the dying awaken to the preciousness of time, they can noticeably relax into the moment. The spouse of one hospice patient remarked that she could not remember after fifty years of marriage the last time her husband had said he loved her. "Now that his time is limited," she said, "he keeps telling me how much he has always appreciated me." Her husband commented that when he became terminally ill he began to notice her again.

Now that a combination of protease inhibitors and standard antiviral medications have become available, some AIDS patients are discovering a new dilemma. Previously most AIDS patients had a limited prognosis. Now, because of these drugs, some of them are opening to a different perspective on their future. A few find themselves financially compromised because they depleted their incomes as a consequence of their limited life expectancy. Now they find themselves living longer, and time takes on a different meaning.

How do you live when your terminal illness is no longer imminent? This is the same problem most of us have who are healthy. We are all terminally ill, but no one knows for certain when time will end. How do we live with time in a way that neither overreacts nor discounts the fact we are going to die?

The dying can teach us about this dilemma through their unique perspective on time. Time for them is limited. When we observe that something is limited, we develop different assumptions about its value. At first the patients try very hard to have quality time. That usually means they attempt to cram more of their desires into the time remaining. As the patient's energy wanes and they realize they will never do everything they wanted to do, they begin to emphasize the value of their presence in time. Their use of time changes from doing to being.

Ben was always a hard-working man. His wife, Jenny, said she barely saw him on weekdays. He would go to work early and arrive home late in the evening. Ben was proud of the life he had created for Jenny, which he credited to his long working hours. Jenny, however, complained about their lack of quality time together. She said there were very few occasions in all the years of marriage that were devoted to building their relationship.

Then Ben became ill with cancer. At first he did everything he could to cure himself, but nothing worked. The doctor told him he only had months to live. Ben decided he and Jenny would take the Hawaiian vacation they had planned after his retirement. But Jenny told Ben she did not want to go to Hawaii; she said she wanted to spend time with him alone, without distraction. Jenny said Ben did not understand what she wanted him to do. Later in his illness, as he became confined to bed, Ben started to call Jenny to him and whisper the depth of his affection in her ear. He did this many times a day. Sometimes he would call her and just hold her hand. Jenny said she appreciated him more during those final days than she ever had in their marriage.

Sometimes we miss the love we have for each other in our busyness. Death is the ending of time. We can no longer divert ourselves from opening our hearts. This ending of time can allow us to return to caring. It is found in the balance between overreacting to the fact of our death

and denying it will occur at all. Those of us who feel we have plenty of
time seem to fracture our lives into different time commitments. Caring
gets squeezed in between our obligations and our responsibilities. This
creates an artificial division between our duties and our hearts. Death
speaks to this division and split.

FRACTURED TIME

Time is one aspect of our lives that seems completely beyond our control. It marches endlessly in one direction, dragging us along with it.
It seems to work more against us than for us. In this culture, with our
emphasis on efficiency and precision, we live under the pressure of the
clock. Time threatens us with consequences if we fail to act: our boss
will be upset, or we will miss the train. Like the white rabbit that Alice
encountered in Wonderland, who was always running with his watch in
hand, time is often a source of fear and anxiety.

We often speak about time as if we could control it. We talk about
wasting and saving it as if time were a product we could purchase and
own. But is time something to be gained or consumed like our other
possessions? Dying patients frequently ask how much time they have
left. The question can be a source of anxiety because the answer relates
to life in terms of measured time.

Depending upon the circumstances of the moment, time can be seen
either as an enemy or as a friend. In either case our relationship with it is
one of struggle. Either it goes by too quickly, as we attempt to prolong a
pleasant occasion, or it drags on when we react to the situation as boring
or distressing. We either like the time we are in or we do not. Even when
we are having a good time, we may not be content. More than likely,
we are trying to have an even better time. We all seem to be seeking the
moment when, as the beer commercial proclaims, "It just doesn't get
any better than this!" All of this leads to a pervasive sense of discontent
and restlessness. This moment is rarely good enough on its own.

Sometimes we attempt to postpone or delay the present time by not
thinking about it. The current time can be so laced with anxiety and
difficulty we simply relocate our thoughts in another time frame. We

mentally take ourselves out of the moment we live in and withdraw into an imaginary time. This leads to procrastination and denial. Our bodies remain in one location and our minds in another. When we procrastinate, we delay the discomfort and carry it over into a future time, saying, "I'll do it later." When we deny, we are choosing to live in another time, a time before the tumor, or when our husband or wife was still alive.

I worked with a ninety-seven-year-old woman who was dying of cancer. She always had a nice home and plenty of money to spend on whatever she needed. Her physical deterioration was a shock to her. She simply did not believe she was going to die. During one of my later visits, when her weakness was increasing and she was realizing death was imminent, she looked up and said, "Why me? Why now?"

We can live our whole life in a fictitious time that does not contain death. This woman lived ninety-seven years and wondered why death was happening to her. Where had she been? At what age would death have been appropriate? Death did not have any place whatsoever in her time scheme. She lived in one time frame, death in another. Living in a different time frame from aging, dying, and death eventually brought her a great deal of mental anguish.

The discord associated with carving death out from time does not stop with psychological unhappiness. When we excise death, time cannot teach us its lessons. We coerce time to live by our rules. The difference between living in a time that contains death and one that does not is the difference between being spiritually alive or dead. Christ pointed this out when he said, "Stay forever awake, for the Kingdom of God is at hand." We are awake only when we are living within current time and not fabricating an imaginary one. Christ is admonishing us to relocate ourselves in this present moment—a moment that, like all moments, includes death.

There are many ways we use time to dislocate ourselves from reality and prevent a proper alignment of our mind and body experience. All of these create various forms of self-inflicted suffering. We fracture our lives into discrete times. We have work time, play time, alone time, meal time, family time, and so on. If one of these infringes upon another, we may become upset. For example, if our children interrupt our alone time or we get a call from work while we are eating, we consider it an intrusion. We see our time as being compartmentalized; now it is time for this, now it is time for that. Anything that disturbs or crosses over these boundaries can create conflict and impatience.

When we fracture time, we fracture ourselves. Each time we separate one time interval (alone time) from another (family time) we divide ourselves into separate persons. The person who wants time by himself is in conflict with the person who feels he must relate to his family. Each person has a different sense of role and different expectations and needs. For instance, if we are driving to an appointment and get caught in a traffic jam, we push against this time interval: "I need to get there now!" We can become startlingly aggressive because in our rush we become victims of time. Time becomes an imposition, a stressor working against our welfare. When time is a stressor, it forces a division within us. In this instance there are two people competing in the car. There is the one who sits stuck in the traffic and the one who wants to be at the appointment. The two are in conflict.

When we view time in this fractured way, we place ourselves outside of life and life outside of time. At some point most of us have felt as if we were outside life looking in, as if we were a bystander to our living experience. When we place ourselves out of time, we feel as if time is something happening to us. Time feels like an external stream carrying us along in its wake. When we are outside of time we are outside of life as well. On these occasions we are struggling with our immediate time frame, either living in some imaginary future or past or struggling desperately with the interval we are in.

Life, time, and we ourselves are all one and the same event, not three things operating independently. As Thich Nhat Hanh has said, "All time is our time." Time in a traffic jam is as much our time as time alone or time with our children. We cannot waste or save time; there is just time. Where are its boundaries? All time is happening simultaneously. We misjudge our experience if we believe that different events occur in their own separate compartments of time. Life is time, and I, too, am time.

In her diary one of our hospice patients writes, "What a day! First my Timmy [her twelve-year-old grandson] came to visit. I love him so. He is so busy. No time for his sick grandma! ... Sarah [a neighbor] also came over. I see her so differently now. Her nervousness kept me from listening before. She really is a dear. ... All these visitors, I just sit back and let them come. I appreciate them all, but I especially like being by myself. But I get plenty of aloneness. It is there for the asking."

Time becomes integrated into who we are when we no longer split it into isolated pieces. It no longer presses in or causes anxiety because it is never in opposition to our aliveness. We settle into a deep, abiding contentment, a contentment that comes from seeing time holistically. All the separate times that have pulled us this way and that come together. We participate in life as it comes and goes. Nothing special, nowhere else to be. Our pace slows, but not our acuity and clarity. All conflict ends between time intervals because everything is experienced in the present.

INTEGRATING INTO TIME PRESENT

One of our hospice patients made a prediction about his own death. As he was becoming weaker and confined to his bed he suddenly stated to his family that he would be dead before Wednesday. He died five minutes before midnight on Tuesday night. His wife said she fully expected him to live up to his prophecy. "He was always punctual in life," she said. "I saw no reason to believe he would be different in keeping his appointment with death."

Hospice staff often observe their patients developing an unusual relationship to time as death approaches. It is quite common for patients to wait until loved ones arrive from distant places before they decide to die. The opposite can also be true. The patients may wait until their loved one, who has been by their bed night and day, leaves the room. They then die alone in a room that is quiet and silent. It is clear the dying have some degree of choice in the time they die. They seem to be able to postpone the moment of their death until certain conditions are met.

Marilyn, a patient I served, had many loving children and grandchildren attending her throughout her long illness. One morning, when everyone was entering and leaving Marilyn's room in a confusing and crowded way, she came out of her nearly comatose state and called everyone to her bedside. Marilyn asked everyone to do something for her that would force them to leave her room. One person was asked to get her some ice water, another to pick up some medications, and so on, until each person including me had a task. We all left, and after finishing our chores we reassembled in her room to find Marilyn had died in our absence.

How did this woman and the many like her manage to manipulate time and delay her death? The dying often have a completely different relationship to the present time. No longer pushing against one moment to get into the next or attempting to carry this moment into the future, they are integrated with time. They learn to live within the moment, and time begins to work with them in a cooperative way.

Sometimes the dying connect with other realities within time. They talk and converse with people who have died before them, who are unseen from our time perspective. Like Marilyn, they frequently have a strong intuitive sense of how to use time, an awareness that defies conventional understanding. Their powers of observation also increase as they become more and more sensitive to the subtleties of the moment. Their eyes brighten, and there can be great clarity and wisdom.

Eliminating the pressure of time is the key to integrating into the moment. The dying often settle into time in a way that few of us do. Tomorrow has been taken away. All they have, with any assurance at all, is now. Having only now allows them to be free from the bondage of the future. There is nothing left but this immediate moment, where life is still active and vital regardless of how close to death they happen to be.

We are taken away from the immediate process of living when we project our life into the future. Living in an abstract future forces a gaining or striving relationship with time. We fill the future with our imagination and then run toward it as if it were real. We want things that are not available and cannot be easily obtained. One hospice patient said he did not realize how much time he spent thinking about the next thing he had to do until, confined to bed, he was unable to do anything. He said he understood for the first time how much energy he wasted on worrying about something that never occurred.

Most of us believe the future will happen according to our plans. We were alive yesterday, and we believe we will be alive tomorrow. It is undeniable that plans must be made, but many of us live with a false sense of reality regarding the certainty of those plans. We live as if tomorrow were actually occurring today. Mentally we project our present moment into a certain future. One of the reasons we are so shocked when a tragedy hits is that our projected future does not contain any deviations from our present safety. We find it difficult to live without creating an assured future because in doing so we eliminate the uncertainty of time.

And what about the past, with all of its memories, remorse, and grief? It is the historical luggage that we tow into present relationships. The past colors almost everything our senses perceive in this moment. We look at an object and see our history with it. We recognize its name, shape, color, and utility all from our past. We then begin to relate to it with reference to the past. If we liked it in the past, we are prepared to welcome it now. If not, we reject it. This is how we view almost everything in life including ourselves.

The past demands attention because we feel its influence. It keeps waking us to the pain of our past indiscretions and reminding us of our lack of self-forgiveness. The unforgiving past holds us in judgment, refusing to allow us to move beyond. It is as if we continue to look in the rearview mirror to check our currect position. Our backs bend with the weight of the sorrow we carry.

Death halts the forward and backward movement of time. It brings time to an end. The dying often realize this abrupt ending and attempt to settle themselves with their past before death arrives. Some find themselves reliving their traumatic past. One woman relived her childbirths again and again; another patient had flashbacks to his involvement in World War II.

One poignant illustration of this occurred in our hospice program with Herb, a patient who had been an alcoholic and severely abusive to his family throughout much of his married life. As Herb came closer to death he attempted to reconcile his past behavior with his wife and children. After all the physical and verbal abuse the family had tolerated, they could offer very little forgiveness to Herb. The patient started to have daily nightmares in which he dreamed he was being tortured by someone who was intoxicated. Herb would scream out from his sleep asking his tormentor to "please stop . . . please stop." His family said those were the very words they used when they pleaded for an end to their own abuse from Herb.

Herb was working very hard to square himself with his past. He could not postpone this important work any longer. His death would not permit it. Herb's past demanded his attention in ways he had avoided in health. It haunted his subconscious until through his dreams he took responsibility for his actions. Perhaps through these long nightmares there was some respite for Herb from his past and the beginning of self-forgiveness.

The problem that most of us face in integrating into the moment is understanding our thoughts. Time is created from our thinking. The past and the future are simply streams of thoughts about something that has occurred or has yet to occur. These thoughts create the illusion of actual time. Even when we arrive in the present from this mental time travel, we look through our thoughts into the present moment. We experience this moment through the thought of what we would like it to be or through the thought of what we are afraid it will become. We find it difficult to reconcile time the way it is because we expend so much effort rearranging the moment with our thinking.

When we relate to the present through our thoughts, we forsake the experience of being alive and substitute a life of concepts and ideas. It is useful to remember that all thoughts come out of the current activities of the mind. The enormous burden of time travel ends within the simple ground of experience. Thoughts and time are seen for what they are. Even the sense of "I," which substantiates itself in a remembered past and an imagined future, merges into the aliveness of the moment. Here is true forgiveness, true contentment, and true timelessness.

Understanding Your Relationship to Time

Reflect on how you fracture your time into different intervals throughout the day. Do you feel that one interval intrudes upon another? For example, do you resent the time at work because it is time away from your family? Think about all the time you feel is wasted throughout your day. What do you mean by wasted time? Is it time you wanted for more important things? Reflect on whether time is actually divided in these multiple ways.

For one week, practice making every moment "your time," no matter what your activity. Consider the time spent on all the mundane and uncomfortable things you do throughout the day as your own personal time in which you happen to be doing unpleasant things. Time with your family, time at work, time driving your car, time speaking with someone—it is all your private time. What happens to the artificial divisions between your roles and responsibilities and your private time? Experience the way we create needless conflict in our division of time.

Reflect on how much time you spend dwelling on the future, whether planning, daydreaming, or worrying about something that might occur. Reflect on how many of the things you think about really deserve so much mental energy. How many of them ever actually occur? Certain events need to be planned, but do you spend too much time planning? Is worrying a part of the planning? Think about why you do this. What benefit does it give you? How does it limit your possibilities?

Spend a period of time every day watching your thoughts around future events. Label those thoughts "planning," "worrying," "daydreaming," or whatever label comes to you easily. When you catch your mind engaged in future events, reconnect with the actual moment you are living. Ground yourself in the sounds and physical sensations of life as it is happening now. See what happens to those anticipated events as you stay in the present moment.

Reflect on the time you spend dwelling on your past. Think about all the energy you expend mulling over past memories, including remorse, guilt, grief, or some special occasion or event you cannot let go of—an old boyfriend or girlfriend who broke up with you, perhaps, or some event that was held in your honor. Reflect on the difficulty of letting go—of what could have been as well as what was.

For five minutes each day, stand in front of a full-length mirror. See what the mirror sees. Does the mirror see your past? Does it reflect your lack of confidence, your unworthiness, your guilt, or your inhibitions? These accumulations from the past color how you see yourself but not how the world sees you. The world sees only what is reflected in the moment. Go out and live only what the world sees. Let the past go. Keep renewing yourself through the image of the mirror. Refuse to believe that you are in bondage to the past. Releasing yourself from the past in this way may feel awkward or pretentious at first, but it is a more accurate picture of who you are than the one that comes from identifying with the past.

Reflect on the value of living in the present moment. How much of your time is spent in the present as opposed to maintaining your fantasies and memories? How would your life be different if you learned to be more deeply connected to each moment? There are many audiotapes, videotapes, and books that give very good instructions on mindfulness meditation. Reflect on your death, and ask yourself what is stopping you from involving yourself in one of these practices.

For thirty minutes each day, sit quietly and practice mindfulness meditation. Obtain an instructional tape if necessary, and dedicate yourself to the practice for three months. Keep a journal, and at the end of the three months, but not before, evaluate the practice. Observe your day-to-day living experiences, your relationships, your states of mind, and ask yourself if the meditation practice is making a difference in your life. Answer honestly, and then choose to continue to practice or not.

14 | The Deathless

Because we die our death in this life, because
we are continually taking leave, continually
disappointed, ceaselessly piercing through realities
into their nothingness, continually narrowing the
possibilities of free choice through our actual decisions
and actual life ... we die throughout life, and what we
call death is really the end of death, the death of death.
—KARL RAHNER

UNDERSTANDING THE DECEPTION of past and future time leads us into the final lesson of death. Death does not occur within time. The dying seem to go through time to a place that time cannot touch. The body is dead, it is still. Time has come to an end. What is there before we were born? What is there after we have died? These are questions that evoke mystery and point beyond time to complete rest and contentment. In pursuing them, we discover the ultimate wisdom of the dying.

If we raise these questions at all, it is usually when we are very old or ill. The voices of the dying are a constant reminder of this wisdom imparted throughout life and accessible to everyone. It is the wisdom of our ancestors, recognized by young children intrigued by the wrinkled skin and deep-set eyes of their grandparents. Although aging and death are incomprehensible to the child's mind, there is often an inexplicable attraction between the very young and the very old. As children, in our innocence, we sense that our grandparents know something greater, something that is beyond our comprehension. So we ask them questions: "What was it like when you were young, Grandma? How did you get around without airplanes?" The answers, though interesting, do not really touch the depth of our questions. We are searching for their wisdom. We want to know about all those years of life experience. We are inquiring into ourselves. We want to know if they can teach us how to live.

The dying take us straight to those answers. To look into the face of death is to bypass all the idle prattle that keeps us from gazing into the eyes of the nursing home patient. If we can withstand the climb, suddenly our viewpoint becomes one of great expansiveness. From our elevation, we see everything in new perspective. The wisdom of the dying becomes our wisdom. Our lives become richer and more meaningful, freer and more spacious.

When we live according to the mandates of death, we live a life of freedom. Death is the way to live. It reveals what is true and false by eliminating everything unreliable. Whatever changes is in transition to something else and is therefore unstable. Everything in the body and mind is in transition. We cannot rest our identity upon something that will eventually be taken away. Only what is unalterable can be the Truth, not what dies. The Truth is ever itself, or it would not be true; and death, the absolute ending of the transitory, discloses it.

Because death reveals the Truth it also guides us to it. It is a spiritual blueprint of how to live according to the way things are. It is all the spiritual teaching we will ever need. If we are sincere in our spiritual endeavors, everything we do prepares us to meet this teaching. We can easily get lost in the intricate details of our spiritual practice and find ourselves very distant from this final lesson. Then suddenly we begin to die, and we wonder where we have gone astray. How has our spiritual practice been relevant to our impending death?

We should be cautious when the course of our growth deviates very far from death. We can fool ourselves into thinking that we were going toward something more important, but our spiritual growth leads us toward nothing. If our spiritual practice leaves us with the residue of an accomplishment or if we find ourselves becoming proud and boastful about our spiritual faculties, we can steer ourselves back on course by realigning our practices with death.

Many of us idle away our time with elaborate forms of meditation and ritual far from the truth of death. Our spiritual practices, if they do not direct us toward death, risk becoming subtle forms of spiritual entertainment that lull us to sleep, and we become oblivious to the critical issue of self-understanding. Such practices can actually be counterproductive. We may think we are growing spiritually while actually we are reinforcing conditioned patterns of fear and selfishness. Death, however, only waits so long before forcing its lesson upon us. Death is the school of the one hard knock.

The knock of death confirms there is no place to hide, no place to rest because everything is in transition toward something else. We spend much of our lives seeking a refuge from the storm of death only to find our cloister disintegrating in time. Our minds, bodies, roles, responsibilities, relationships, accomplishments, self-images—everything goes with time. Death says, "Build something up, but keep an eye on me. I have the final word." Death holds us to that word.

We usually place all our attention on building up and forget to keep an eye on death. This is disastrous for our well-being because the building and the dying are one and the same. Milarepa, the renowned Tibetan yogi, was instructed by his teacher to build stone houses one day and dismantle them the next. He did this day after day until the lessons of death merged with life. Building up and destroying are two views of the same incident. Death is occurring in each moment of life. We are not the same person we were a moment ago, nor does anything in the universe maintain itself for even an instant. It all falls continuously into the cavern of death.

LIVING OUR DEATH

Many people who are on the edge of their lives seem to know a secret. They reveal those secrets through their conversations, their dreams, their visions. But mostly they reveal the power of their secret by the way they die. Many make the actual moment of death look easy. It almost seems anticlimactic to the viewer, nothing special at all. It is only when we live with death in full view that this "nothing special" secret can be imparted to us. Death becomes another moment of life, and our whole life is made easier in its recognition.

To live our death means we do not project continuity onto our experiences. We invite death into the moment by allowing the moment to die. We do not prolong the moment beyond its natural duration. Everything is allowed to be just as it is. Death then merges into the moment itself. It becomes the moment. It creates aliveness within the moment by constantly turning over fresh soil, bringing forth the new and the mysterious. We meet death in this aliveness without separation or differentiation.

Living our death occurs when there is no separation between ourselves and dying. It occurs when dying is not made into something apart from living. Death is no longer the ultimate point of reference for our fear. We are not closer to it as we age, nor are we farther away in our youth. We no longer use death as a measurement to define our present health and well-being. Death is equally present across the entire spectrum of space and time. It is not a problem for us when there is no us apart from death. There is just what is. With the integration of the person into what is, the distinction between the person and death ends.

Death enters our hearts unimpeded when we open to life as it is, and with this opening comes the innocence of silence. That innocence arrives in its full flowering when we say, I do not know. It comes when we no longer cover the world with our explanations. It comes when we have tired of our imagination. The Buddha was once asked how you authenticate the Truth. He said, "Do not say, 'This is the way it is.'" In the absence of our certainty arrives the life of innocence. When we are not focused on creating differences, we are free to notice what everything has in common.

Death comes through the silence at the end of an answer when there is nothing else to ask. It comes in the still space between our thoughts. It arrives in the moment of quiet receptivity when our hearts are not protecting what we know. Death is found when we listen so completely that the distinction between helper and helped is forgotten. It is in the small acts of kindness that are performed without pride, in the acts of love committed for the sake of love. It is in the simple deeds of generosity that come from an open heart. It was there when the dying nine-year-old girl reached beyond her pain to comfort her grief-stricken father.

Joseph Campbell once described Carl Jung as a man "grounded in eternity and moving in time." Jesus was pointing to this quality in a person when he said, "Be in the world but not of the world." It is possible to live in time but be rooted in the timeless. Such a person embodies death. She is simply herself without any trace of self-doubt. She exists before the formation of her psychic shadow where death no longer stalks life. She is exceptional only in the fact of her total lack of pretension. A description of one highly regarded Zen teacher reads, "in the end it is not the extraordinariness of the teacher that perplexes . . . the student, it is the teacher's utter ordinariness."

As these examples illustrate, to embody death while we live means we return to the roots of our beginning. As T. S. Eliot wrote in the Four Quartets, "And the end of all our exploring will be to arrive where we started and know the place for the first time." No special hoopla or hyperbole. One who walks in death dwells in the simplicity of his own humanity. Such a person understands the limits of time by never placing himself outside time. He is grounded in the deathless.

FROM DEATH TO THE DEATHLESS

Death beckons our spiritual hearts. It is at the root of our longing to return. Its call is the call of ages, of a time long since forgotten when we were free in our naturalness and born to quietude. We have long been afraid to be who we are. Death will take away everything we think we possess to show us in an instant the ground of our being. What is left is beyond the reach of death.

Countering the flow of worldly life, death puts an end to all gain and accumulation. It backs us up to the beginning and drops us at birth's door. The crying this time, however, is not from the pains of birth but from the suffering of having to let go. Death reminds us that we are born to let go. We come in with nothing, and we go out with nothing. In between we attempt to elude this nothing by amassing wealth and knowledge, but these have little to do with life at either end. Life has always been about nothing despite our best efforts to the contrary. This nothing, however, is not an empty despondency or vacuity; rather it is a profound description of who we really are.

Death takes the self away. The body and brain both go, leaving us with nothing to call our own. All expressions of our individuality are over. Everything we related to as "I" has died. Who are we after death? We do not become somebody when we die. We become nobody. This is perhaps death's greatest teaching. It directs us to the truth of what we have always been. The "I" and "me" die with death. Death eliminates our sense of separation. What is left after death is common to us all.

Understanding this is both humbling and ennobling; we perceive a potential that few of us have realized. Death speaks to something more profound than our self-imposed limitations. We cannot carry our identity with us as we go, for death is bigger than anyone, bigger than the king or the beggar, the genius or the simpleton. Wealth and status have no bearing. We go beyond who we are to a hidden promise known only to death and to those who live their death while alive.

Death consumes all conditioned things; nothing that relies on conditions escapes it. But is there something that does not rely on conditions? If there were, it would exist before birth and have no qualities or characteristics, because all qualities are subject to change. It would not be observable by the senses and therefore could not be seen, heard, smelled, tasted, or touched. It would not be provable to the mind because the mind knows only that which exists in time. Unlimited by time, it would be unmoving, unchanging, and undying.

Death points toward that which is beyond conditions. Its very nature confirms the eternal. Death is complete stillness into which all things must fall. In the instant of death there is an absolute ending of all movement. Therefore death is beyond movement. When something dies, it stops, and its deathless nature is revealed.

The conditioned objects of the world are the deathless in a disguised state. Our minds keep things moving within time; in the deathless they are not moving at all. We do not see what is; we see what has been or what will be. We look at the world as caught between the past and the future. We assess what is in front of us, looking ahead to see how we can manipulate it, or we relate to things with the grief-stricken eyes of what used to be. We color all that exists with our past history and future expectations. Nothing is allowed to reveal itself to us because we impose time upon it. When time is removed, death is eliminated, and everything falls into the deathless.

We miss this common element because of our fears and desires. Our aversion and wanting makes things out of no-things. We hold things to what we want them to be and do not allow them to be the way they are. But death continually intercedes in our thing-making and eliminates these entities from view. In so doing, death demonstrates that what we thought was true never was, and it continually reveals the real Truth, which is forever unchanged. Instead of delighting in this revelation, we mourn and weep the passing of these imaginary separate things.

In a photograph, the picture and the paper are one and the same thing. When we focus on the forms in the photograph, we ignore the paper. We see the images as if they were a depiction of reality, and we do not notice the paper until we have tired of the images. Similarly, when we set aside our need to acquire and hold on to the individual expressions of life, we are available to see what supports life itself. The deathless has always been here. We have chosen to ignore it and enjoy only the images.

All forms of life rest in the deathless. We are so busy building up and focusing on the figure we forget the ground. The deathless ground on which all things are based does not move. We move on the ground. This moment, which we call time, is the movement of our thoughts. We think about where we have been and where we are going, bringing the past and future into almost everything we do. We look at life and see what we want or what we fear.

The moment of physical death is the intersection between time and the timeless, a portal through all of this movement that offers us a glimpse of the ground on which we have been moving. The clouds part, and suddenly we see the sun. Death holds the extraordinary possibility of seeing life without the interference of time, which is why it is revered by many spiritual traditions. It is a single instant in which there is no movement. Everything is stripped away, and nothing remains in motion.

This is why the message of death brings freedom. Eternally true, death reveals the error we make in losing ourselves in time. The moment of death can unveil the timeless. Our whole life has brought us to this benediction. It is the parting blessing that life offers to partake in the freedom we have so long avoided. In this sense, death is grace. A gift from life to become life. Like all gifts the recipient must be ready to receive. Every action we have taken, everything we have ever done either prepares us to receive this gift or pass it by. As one hospice patient said, "I don't know what is ahead for me, but I am going to keep my eyes wide open."

In near-death experiences, the ground—the deathless—is usually seen as an all-consuming light. But to observe it as light still means we are operating within the sphere of our conditioned senses. Fundamentally all life is this ground, and to truly be it we cannot be observing it. Our wanting to observe and understand death is our attempt to make it safe and palatable. But we cannot bargain with the ground. It is all or nothing. It either consumes us totally with no trace remaining or it is missed completely. We cannot flutter around God like a moth around a lamp. Either we are in Truth or we are out of it. Either we squirm with death or we die into the deathless.

In every action there is an opportunity to die. In every movement there is the possibility of stopping. Death is not merely the moment of time when our body stops. It exists within all moments of time. We deny death whenever there is any movement away from this moment whatsoever. The Tao Te Ching says, "The secret waits for eyes unclouded by longing." Any imaginary reality created in time, any impulse toward desire and fear, any resistance to life at all, and heaven and earth are infinitely far apart. With the slightest movement of mind, a world is created that is afraid to die, and the deathless is lost within time.

All movement within time is a denial of death, for death is nonmovement and complete rest. We confine ourselves within mental activity in order to avoid seeing any sign of our impending demise. It is even hard for us to sit still and do nothing, for such quietude intimates inward stillness. To be quiet strikes too close to the truth of our mortality.

Our spiritual practice must be based in nonmovement if we are to resurrect death. To grow spiritually is to foster a relationship with death—to bring it in, uncover it, and become it. What does it mean to be completely still? What is left after everything dies? The approach of physical death impels us to these questions, whose answers we can uncover in our spiritual growth.

The great message of death is the message of the timeless, of infinity, of mystery. If we hold death only within our thoughts, then the truth of death is obscured by what we want it to be. We must, instead, go through death and become death itself. We must enter into death, become one with the stillness of death. Death's message is one of hope and love, for it points the way to the very fulfillment of life, not to its diminishment. We study death in order to learn how to live.

It is said that when Plato was very near death a friend asked him to summarize his life work, *The Dialogues*. Plato came out of a coma to answer. He looked at his friend and said simply, "Practice dying."

Further Reading

BOOKS ON DEATH AND DYING:

Borysenko, Joan. *Fire in the Soul: A New Psychology of Spiritual Optimism.* New York: Warner, 1994.

Byock, Ira. *Dying Well.* New York: Riverhead, 1997.

Cassell, Eric. *The Nature of Suffering.* New York: Oxford University Press, 1991.

Kelley, Patricia, and Maggie Callanan. *Final Gifts.* New York: Bantam, 1993.

Kessler, David. *The Rights of the Dying: A Companion of Life's Final Moments.* New York: HarperCollins, 1997.

Kübler-Ross, Elisabeth. *Death: The Final Stage of Growth.* New York: Simon & Schuster, 1975.

——*On Death and Dying.* New York: Collier, 1970.

Levine, Stephen. *Meetings on the Edge: Dialogues with the Grieving and the Dying, the Healing and the Healed.* New York: Anchor Doubleday, 1989.

——*Who Dies? An Investigation of Conscious Living.* New York: Anchor Doubleday, 1982.

——*A Year to Live: How to Live This Year As If It Were Your Last.* New York: Random House, 1997.

Nuland, Sherwin. *How We Die.* New York: Vintage, 1994.

Sogyal Rinpoche. *The Tibetan Book of Living and Dying.* San Francisco: HarperSanFrancisco, 1992.

Ufema, Joy. *Brief Companions.* Fawn Grove, PA: The Mulligan Company, 1984.

Wilber, Ken. *Grace and Grit: Spirituality and Healing in the Life and Death of Treya Killam Wilber.* Boston: Shambhala, 1993.

BOOKS ON GRIEF:

Doka, Kenneth. *Children Mourning, Mourning Children*. Hemisphere, 1995.

Ericsson, Stephanie. *Companion through the Darkness*. New York: HarperCollins, 1993.

Kelley, Patricia. *Companion to Grief: Finding Consolation When Someone You Love Dies*. New York: Simon & Schuster, 1997.

Neeld, Elizabeth Harper. *Seven Choices*. New York: Dell, 1990.

Rapaport, Nessa. *A Woman's Book of Grieving*. New York: William Morrow, 1994.

Tatelbaum, Judy. *The Courage to Grieve: Creative Living, Recovery and Growth through Grief*. New York: HarperCollins, 1984.

Viorst, Judith. *Necessary Losses*. New York: Ballantine, 1987.

RESOURCE BOOKS ON MEDITATION AND SELF-AWARENESS:

Boorstein, Sylvia. *Don't Just Do Something, Sit There*. San Francisco: Harper San Francisco, 1996.

——*It's Easier Than You Think: The Buddhist Way to Happiness*. San Francisco: Harper San Francisco, 1997.

Buddhadāsa Bhikkhu. *Mindfulness with Breathing*. Boston: Wisdom, 1996.

Feldman, Christina. *Woman Awake*. London: Arkana, 1990.

Goldstein, Joseph. *The Experience of Insight: A Simple and Direct Guide to Buddhist Meditation*. Boston: Shambhala, 1987.

——*Insight Meditation: The Practice of Freedom*. Boston: Shambhala, 1994.

Goldstein, Joseph, and Jack Kornfield. *Seeking the Heart of Wisdom: The Path of Insight Meditation*. Boston: Shambhala, 1987.

Gunaratana, Henepola. *Mindfulness in Plain English*. Boston: Wisdom, 1993.

Hanh, Thich Nhat. *Being Peace*. Berkeley: Parallax, 1996.

Harrison, Gavin. *In the Lap of the Buddha*. Boston: Shambhala, 1994.

Kabat-Zinn, Jon. *Wherever You Go There You Are: Mindfulness Meditation in Everyday Life*. New York: Hyperion, 1994.

Keating, Thomas. *Open Mind, Open Heart: The Contemplative Dimension of the Gospel*. Rockport, MA: Element, 1992.

Khema, Ayya. *Being Nobody, Going Nowhere: Meditations on the Buddhist Path*. Boston: Wisdom, 1987.

——*Who Is My Self? A Guide to Buddhist Meditation*. Boston: Wisdom, 1987.

Kornfield, Jack. *A Path with Heart: A Guide through the Perils and Promises of Spiritual Life*. New York: Bantam, 1993.

——*Teachings of Twelve Buddhist Masters*. Boston: Shambhala, 1995.

Krishnamurti, J. *Freedom from the Known*. New York: Harper & Row, 1969.

Merton, Thomas. *The Wisdom of the Desert*. New York: New Direction, 1960.

Noh, Jae Jah. *Do You See What I See?* London: Quest, 1977.

Salzberg, Sharon. *A Heart as Wide as the World: Living with Mindfulness, Wisdom, and Compassion*. Boston: Shambhala, 1997.

——*Lovingkindness: The Revolutionary Art of Happiness*. Boston: Shambhala, 1995.

Sumedho, Ajahn. *The Mind and the Way: Buddhist Reflections on Life*. Boston: Wisdom, 1995.

Suzuki, Shunryu. *Zen Mind, Beginner's Mind*. New York: Weatherill, 1973.

Tarthang Tulku. *Time, Space, and Knowledge*. Berkeley: Dharma Publishing, 1977.

Titmuss, Christopher. *The Profound and the Profane*. Totnes, England: Insight Books, 1993.

About the Author

 RODNEY SMITH spent eight years in monastic settings both at the Insight Meditation Society in Massachusetts and as a Buddhist monk in Asia. He ordained with Mahāsi Sayadaw in Burma and practiced several years with Ajahn Buddhadāsa at Wat Suan Mok in Thailand. After disrobing as a monk in 1983, he became a full-time hospice worker. He worked over seventeen years as a hospice social worker, bereavement coordinator, program director, and executive director. He currently offers workshops and retreats on end-of-life issues and teaches insight meditation nationally. Rodney is the guiding teacher for the Seattle Insight Meditation Society and Insight Meditation Houston and a senior teacher for the Insight Meditation Society in Barre, Massachusetts.

About Wisdom Publications

WISDOM PUBLICATIONS is the leading publisher of classic and contemporary Buddhist books and practical works on mindfulness. Publishing books from all major Buddhist traditions, Wisdom is a nonprofit charitable organization dedicated to cultivating Buddhist voices the world over, advancing critical scholarship, and preserving and sharing Buddhist literary culture.

To learn more about us or to explore our other books, please visit our website at www.wisdompubs.org. You can subscribe to our eNewsletter, request a print catalog, and find out how you can help support Wisdom's mission either online or by writing to:

Wisdom Publications
199 Elm Street
Somerville, Massachusetts 02144 USA

You can also contact us at 617-776-7416 or info@wisdompubs.org.

Wisdom is a 501(c)(3) organization, and donations in support of our mission are tax deductible.

Wisdom Publications is affiliated with the Foundation for the Preservation of the Mahayana Tradition (FPMT).

Also Available from Wisdom Publications

The Arts of Contemplative Care
Pioneering Voices in Buddhist Chaplaincy and Pastoral Work
Cheryl A. Giles, Willa B. Miller
Foreword by Judith Simmer-Brown
Hardcover
368 pages, $34.95, ebook $24.99

"Destined to become the core text of Buddhist chaplaincy."
—Noah Levine, author of *Dharma Punx*

Buddhist Care for the Dying and Bereaved
Jonathan S. Watts, Yoshiharu Tomatsu
312 pages, $22.95, ebook $16.72

"A valuable and amazing resource! This collection is a 'must' for those of us involved in chaplaincy care."—Pat Enkyo O'Hara, Guiding Teacher, New York Zen Center for Contemplative Care

Dying with Confidence
A Tibetan Buddhist Guide to Preparing for Death
Anyen Rinpoche
Foreword by Tulku Thondup
192 pages, $16.95, ebook $12.35

"A powerful guidebook and a source of comfort at life's most crucial moment."—Tulku Thondup Rinpoche, author of *Boundless Healing*

The Grace in Aging

Awaken as You Grow Older
Kathleen Dowling Singh
240 pages, $17.95, ebook $11.99

"In her wonderful book, Kathleen Dowling Singh helps us to face and embrace the hard truth of the precarious nature of our life. Through her skillful guidance we come to see that aging can be a time of grace and great aliveness."—Frank Ostaseki, founder, Metta Institute

How to Be Sick

A Buddhist-Inspired Guide for the Chronically Ill and Their Caregivers
Toni Bernhard
Foreword by Sylvia Boorstein
216 pages, $15.95, ebook $11.62

"Full of hopefulness and promise . . . this book is a perfect blend of inspiration and encouragement. Toni's engaging teaching style shares traditional Buddhist wisdom in a format that is accessible to all readers."—*The Huffington Post*

Zen Cancer Wisdom

Tips for Making Each Day Better
Daju Suzanne Friedman
320 pages, 5x8", $16.95, ebook $11.99

"Something truly astonishing can happen when we are pushed to the edge of our life. Daju Suzanne Friedman met her cancer diagnosis with the courage of everyday Zen. She leads us through the mundane and the horrific with such steadfast wisdom that her book reminds us what is possible for our lives as we engage the inevitable challenges of old age, sickness, and death."—Rodney Smith, author of *Lessons from the Dying*